SCOTTISH WILDERNESS CONNECTIONS

wandering and wondering
among landscapes and seascapes

Robin Lloyd-Jones

with a preface by
Jay Griffiths

First published 2021
by Rymour Books
45 Needless Road
PERTH
EH1 2JU

© Robin Lloyd-Jones 2021

ISBN 978-1-9196286-7-7

Cover design by Ian Spring
Printed and bound by
Imprint Digital
Seychelles Farm
Upton Pyne
Exeter

The paper used in this book is approved
by the Forest Stewardship Council

CONTENTS

FOREWORD

This book is a mosaic; built of small and colourful parts, it creates a portrait of nature in many forms. From the colours of the Clyde, with its pewters, slates and platinums, to night kayaking with Lloyd-Jones. Walking in Scottish glens or paddling into MacKinnon's Cave.

It includes an unusual menu which details Mummery's Blood – W H Murray's concoction of hot rum and Bovril – and a description of how to make Guddled Trout: 'first tickle Your trout, as a well-tickled trout goes into a trance and can be lifted out of the water'. An essay entitled 'In Praise of Small Islands' introduces us to the Sacred Isle of the Moon, a tiny island on Loch Maree, where, perhaps with the lunar-lunatic connection, a person suffering mental illness could be cured, it was said, by being towed around the island behind a boat. At least so it was believed until the late eighteenth century.

And it is a picture of an especial sensibility to the essential world. The author includes an unassuming discussion of his practice of meditation and he writes mindfully of a minded world where empathy extends to everything, from the pools of water in a bog which he memorably describes as 'the moor's upturned eyes' to the last wolf of Sutherland so vivid to him it is as if he saw it: 'a hunted wolf howled, trying in vain to gather his non-existent pack'. His essay on the wolf suggests that to understand humanity we must also understand the wolf: 'Wolf is present in that pull of opposites which sparks our creativity: the need for both order and chaos, for the garden and the forest, safety and danger, freedom and the ties of belonging. Wolf pads through our psyche. He is the craving for mystery, for a sense of otherness, for something elemental and beyond ourselves.'

Landscape is mindscape – it 'has a voice. It shouts, it sings, it murmurs, it whispers' and does so in a multivocal range which the author's acute listening renders for the reader in beautiful prose. Sea is a character in its own right, here, as is River and

Rain.

The author's mind is fluently idiosyncratic as when, for example, he chooses to reinterpret the maxim 'whom the gods love, die young'. In his view, this does not necessarily mean that those beloved of the gods die an early death, but rather could be understood as meaning: 'the gods love those who are still young at heart when they die.' To be young at heart is to be inquisitive, interested and playful; the author is just that. His is a mindscape curiosity-swept and keen with enthusiasm, for art as much as nature; human culture as well as natural culture.

This book is also a true guide book: it suggests and shows by example. It leads the way, or rather leads many ways, for the reader to follow. It invites and encourages you to experience this world on land, on water, in sunlight, in moonlight, outdoors in sweet, especial scenes or indoors in sweet, especial books. Like a good guide, it does not speak in commands, but rather offers, points out a possibility, nods to a route, it suggests and recommends. It whets the whistle, it primes the stove, it itches the toes. This, then, is writing which cannot help itself but to teach, to educate, in its etymology, to lead its readers out into the world, partly through the body – the vivid feeling of the human senses rippling at their most vital in the natural world, and partly through the learning of books and culture. The synthesis of these two is a holistic knowledge which has a natural etiquette of sense and sensitivity; an ethic of appreciation and annotation, of awe and quiet devotion.

JAY GRIFFITHS

Jay Griffiths is an award-winning author of six widely acclaimed books. She is a fierce advocate of nature's remaining wild places. Her book Wild: An Elemental Journey *explores the words and meanings that shape ideas of wildness, arguing that wildness is intrinsic to the health of the human spirit.*

INTRODUCTION

Scottish Wilderness Connections is a collection of my writings, spanning fifty years, about Scottish landscapes and seascapes which have made a deep impression on me. The twenty-four pieces presented here are taken directly or slightly adapted from work previously published or performed: essays, articles, short film scripts, poems, pieces written for my blog and extracts from full-length books; and some have been written especially for this collection. With just a few exceptions they are about Scotland's seas, coastlines, mountains, moors, rivers and forests – a reflection of the fact that Scotland has been my home for over half a century.

My aim in assembling this collection has been to celebrate the beauty I have encountered on foot and by kayak in the great outdoors and to share this joy with others. Three of the pieces are what I term 'praise songs in prose' and it would be true to say that the whole book is a praise song to the wild places I love. The focus, therefore, has been less on my comrades with whom I shared these trips, although, in the totality of the experience, they have been important to me, less on adventure and travel, and more on my own reactions to my surroundings.

I am particularly pleased that *Scottish Wilderness Connections* has given me the opportunity to proclaim the beauty and fascination of Scotland's coastline. Anthologies and collections of writings about landscape and nature have a strangely landlocked attitude. Yet, the Scottish coastline is one of the greatest glories of the British landscape. Because of its highly indented character and multitude of islands, Scotland possesses approximately seventy per cent of Britain's total coastline, a great deal of it consisting of spectacular cliffs and stacks, waterfalls, caves, beautiful sandy bays, wild, wooded shores, exquisite seashells, an abundance of birdlife, colonies of seals and much else besides.

I have also taken the opportunity in this book to describe a few of my explorations of the realms of night, for a place can seem very different once the sun has set. At night we tend to draw the curtains and banish the moon and the stars from our lives, or, if we venture outside, street lights and neon signs pollute the darkness and hide from our vision the wonders of the night sky.

My emphasis on beauty encountered might lead readers to the conclusion that, on matters ecological, I am of the opinion that we have nothing to worry about. This is very far from how I see it. Similarly, I have written of my enjoyment of remote and uninhabited places, and need to say here that behind the valued emptiness often lies the grim history of the Highland Clearances in Scotland. Pollution, deforestation, erosion, diminishing bio-diversity and other problems of our eco-sick planet certainly should be discussed and given prominence. But one slim book cannot do everything. My hope and intention is to point to things worth preserving and to show what we are in danger of losing.

Explorers who visit the remote and beautiful corners of our world are faced with a problem: In telling others about their discoveries do they contribute to the destruction of the very qualities they love about these places? Improved transport, longer holidays and a well-developed tourist industry have created a tidal wave of people eager for a taste of the wilderness. Keeping quiet about our precious finds is no longer an option. Only political will and governmental action at national and international level can now save a large part of Planet Earth's unspoiled areas. Politicians survive by winning votes. Therefore, to raise awareness among the voting public of what we stand to lose has to be the way forward.

In this assortment of writings I make frequent use of the word 'beauty'. I think it important to make two points about that. Firstly I recognise that perception of beauty is a very subjective thing and that it strikes us all in different ways. Secondly it is my belief that all of the natural world is beautiful in its own way, although sometimes we fail to see it. We are trained and conditioned to see one kind of beauty rather than another, or we lack the knowledge to fully grasp the wonder of what is in front of us. This has profound implications in terms of what is deemed worthy of conservation and what is not. Wetlands, for example, are less likely to be protected than what is regarded as a 'classical' landscape; and cuddly or charismatic animals have a better chance of avoiding extinction than less appealing (to us) species.

The American environmentalist, Aldo Leopold, said that recreational development was not a matter of building roads into lovely places, but of building receptivity into the human mind. My hope is that, in some small measure, *Scottish Wilderness Connections* has helped increase that receptivity to the wonders of the natural landscape.

BEINN IME BY MOONLIGHT

It was one thirty in the morning. The road, an empty ribbon of snow, unfolded before our headlights. Helensburgh, Garelochhead, Arrochar – the red mini hummed in and out of people's dreams.

A winter climb by moonlight – I'd waited a long time for this. I had wanted a full moon, snow on the hills, a clear sky, a free weekend. I'd waited 18 years. Hardest of all was the finding of a companion who shared my brand of madness. Once I had set off to do it solo, but in thickening cloud, with rain on the way, I had abandoned the attempt. We topped the rise. Ahead, pale shrouded Beinn-an-Lochain haunted the skyline. The moon was full and bright. Loch Restil lay in frozen trance as Martin engaged a lower gear for the descent into Glen Kinglas.

In the lay-by opposite Butterbridge Burn I consulted the map. The height given for Beinn Ime was 3,318 ft. The brown contour lines and the black hachured cliffs bore no resemblance to the blue-robed monarch at whose feet we sat. I opened the car door. The air bit sharply. More intense even than the cold was the silence. The mountains held their breath; the rushing burns were ice-gripped, the loch in a frozen trance. The glimmering, spell-bound landscape, the feeling of unreality, of time suspended – was it all a dream? We, Martin and I, strapped crampons – twelve-pronged frames – to our boots. To put them on at the roadside, rather than at higher altitude, was a rare event, but then this was the coldest spell Scotland had known for forty years.

'Ready?' I asked, clouds of vapour issuing from my mouth.

Through scarf and Balaclava, Martin gave a muffled, 'Yes.'

Steel-shod boots clanked over the ice-bound burn, then crunched firmly on the mountainside. Ahead, smooth slopes were shimmering like silk. Our shadows flitted before us over the illuminated snow. We crossed wind-rippled, moon-dappled surfaces of sheer delight. We ascended pearl-encrusted, frosted acres which sparkled in a way never seen by day. Above, the hypnotic moon continually drew our gaze. Where our twelve-clawed marks met the tracks of a mountain hare we stopped. Martin grappled with frozen fastenings and produced coffee from a flask. I thought about my warm bed. No! It was here, in this silent realm awash with moonlight, under the stars, that I wanted to be.

Was I imagining it, or did the moon seem yellow-tinged? And was the light now dimmer? The gradient steepened. Between black cliffs long tongues of ice angled towards the summit ridge. The blade of Martin's axe rose and fell. Glittering chips cascaded down the slope. An hour passed. My turn at cutting steps came and went. It was definitely darker. In the excitement of starting out I had forgotten that the moon would set! It slipped below the hills of Inverary and suddenly the mountain was a grimmer place. A chill wind sprang up. Three hundred feet above us the ridge was silhouetted against the sky, while Martin, a few yards away, was barely visible. Secretly, I was glad to be spared the sight of the lengthening drop beneath my heels.

Breathing hard, we gained the ridge. Precipices hinted at their presence on either side. Close by, but how close we couldn't tell, the northern edge would be heavily corniced, the snow overhanging the void by six feet or more. My luminous compass pointed to where the summit ought to be – but we were going downhill! Instinct cried, 'Bear right!' But experience said, 'Trust the compass every time!' And soon the ground took an upward trend. That cornice worried me. I prodded forward with my ice-axe like a blind man with a stick. It was too dangerous to continue in the dark. We knew we must stop and wait for dawn. To escape the wind we dug a hole and cut slabs of hard-packed snow for walls. Inside our makeshift shelter we shivered and waited. Eastwards there was a faint radiation of purple light. Due south, Greenock, Gourock and Dunoon were twinkling bracelets on a black velvet coast, and far, far down the Firth of Clyde, a lighthouse's beam made pin-pricks in the dark.

The last of the coffee; cold prowling; numb toes. A blush was in the sky. Over the shoulder of Ben Lomond crept delicate hues of pink. Slowly, night's dead ashen shapes rekindled in dawn's fire. We stretched stiff limbs, stamped our feet and wandered in disbelief over fields of crimson snow towards our blood-red peak.

It was too cold to stay more than a few minutes at the top. The wind penetrated to the marrow. As we hurried down, range upon range of snow-clad hills were catching the first rays of the sun. Descent was swift. A huge orange ball thrust between two peaks, driving the shadows before us down the valley. I stumbled, then stumbled again. It was twenty-four hours since I had slept.

The last splendorous phase now began. With crampons biting the glinting ice, we walked down the frozen Butterbridge Burn, down cascades frozen into opaque and lumpish shapes; down dense black ice and glass smooth sheets which shone like gold.

The car was in sight. It was seven o'clock. I thought of hot porridge and mugs of coffee. We turned, Martin and I, and gazed at where we'd been. Then we were mere mortals again, with weary legs and one last snowfield to cross.

ARGONAUTS OF THE WESTERN ISLES

At 4am the sun filters through my bedroom window and wakes me. I listen to the Clyde lapping at the lawn and the seabirds calling. I slide my kayak over the dewy grass into the pink dawn water. It glides across the glassy surface. Then, drifting, I hear the plop, plop of fish and watch the sun rise. An hour later I am enjoying mackerel and sea-trout for breakfast, straight from the sea, cooked over a driftwood fire. As I watch the tide-exposed sands striping Craigendoran Bay with bars of gold, I think of the bigger waters beyond the estuary – for the images which surge into my mind and flood my dreams belong to the long summer days kayaking the West Coast of Scotland.

The very first time I experienced an Atlantic swell rolling beneath my kayak and became part of its rhythm I knew I would be returning again and again to those moving hills of water and their deep green valleys. In a fibre-glass shell, inches from the water, there is an intimacy with the sea I have experienced in no other craft: every wave individual, every motion communicated, Man and sea with a minimum of technology between. Learn to handle the double-bladed paddle, study the ocean's moods and rhythms as if she were your lover, and there are few places a kayak cannot go.

Except for the rare days of absolute calm, only a kayak can enter MacKinnon's Cave on Staffa. We battle through the surf into cathedral gloom, basalt columns arching and soaring above us. Fifty yards into the cave it is darker, narrower. Deep, black clefts groan and sigh, panting like the Minotaur. Suddenly a giant swell blots out the entrance. We rise up and up till it explodes around us, booming and echoing. Then, with waterfalls cascading from every ledge, it rushes out again.

And I remember the tranquil moments: Warm nights with the moon laying a silver trail before us; the black silhouette of an island and the scent of wildland wafted on a breeze. On calm days fleets of translucent jellyfish hang like ships in outer space; or one's own zeppelin shadow flits over sandy lagoons and seaweed forests. But, for me, the miles never seem to pass so quickly as when hugging a rocky coastline, following sea-etched ramparts, every yard a marvel of grain and texture and delicate lichens.

A slim, silent kayak creates a minimum of disturbance to marine life. I have glided, unnoticed, close to a feeding otter; porpoises and dolphins have played around us. A kayak can ease amongst a colony of seals without causing alarm; and, if you take a breath and roll upside-down, you can enter their world as they twist and turn around you, so graceful in their proper element.

The birds are different, though. Unused to trespassers near their lonely island cliffs and rocky outcrops, they rise in clouds at our approach. Herring gulls, common gulls and the black-backed ones, cormorants, fulmars, puffins and terns – they circle us, shrieking and swooping, banking into blizzards of white underwing.

Paradise Bay, guarded by rocks and a narrow entrance is accessible only by kayak. It has no other name than the one I gave it. There, in a flower-studded meadow, beside the curving bows of my kayak, I have slept under an orange moon while an otter played in the bay.

There is a pub near Craignish Point where fishermen gather. Now a new breed has arrived. They move their arms differently – elbows in, wrists cocked back, performing imaginary draw-strokes, pawlattas and storm-rolls and looking longingly in the direction of the setting sun. They are the Argonauts of the Western Isles.

MY GOLDEN ISLE

Tides swept me to an isle emerging from the sea.
I laughed and splashed through pools which shone
And end to end made footprints in the sand –
My golden isle, revealed to me alone.
But I forgot that all tides turn,
That loss will follow find.
On dwindling ground I stayed too long,
My tracks dissolving one by one
Till, at the end, I nearly drowned.
Those sands now lie so deep, so many fathoms down.
Can it be? Can it really be?
Will time erase that imprint in the depths of me?

HIGHLAND BURN IN AUTUMN

Beyond my tent pitched on the ridge, ravens float in a crystal chalice of Highland air. Dawn clouds, like drifting windflowers, bloom in shades of pink.

As sunlight chases night down the glen, I follow the burn downstream. Below the snowline it cascades in youthful energy. Granite bowls spill liquid sky. Rock pools brim with splintered light. The burn has cut a small canyon – a gloomy cellar until the climbing sun unlocks caskets of glittering stones and emerald moss. A sheltered lochan glints, unruffled by the breeze.

fish-splash
mountain reflections
vanish

Joined by several tributaries, the burn increases in volume, plunging over a ledge into the pool below. I sit beside the waterfall, observing the unchanging shape of the flow.

tumbling highland burn –
voice and fluid shape of time
ceaselessly reborn

Continuing downhill I pass dappled pools with grained, refracted slabs. The first stunted trees appear along the banks, rowan, hawthorn and mountain ash, their leaves on the turn, forming a ribbon of orange, green and gold winding through a gorge.

Clear of the gorge, the burn merges with a larger flow, meandering towards the ocean where all rivers unite, and where the waters rise again as vapour. Lying on my back in the bracken I watch the sun moves across the sky and suddenly feel that everything is turning: The spinning Earth, the cycle of the seasons; our planet's precious moisture in constant circulation; mountains thrusting upwards, eroding to flat plains, to rise once more; birth, life death and rebirth – wheels within revolving wheels.

The Lord of the Dance
gyrating through endless time
takes me by the hand.

SOUTH UIST BEACH

Joy is a rise of gulls
On a beach in Uist,
Where white dunes, green-topped
Face green waves, white-capped.
Joy is the graceful curve
Of a beach in Uist,
Where a bay's silver sweep
Sisters a pale young moon.
Joy is the harmony
Of a beach in Uist,
Where smooth, sand-scoured bones
Whisper to time-scarred hills.

WHOM THE GODS LOVE

I want to write of the moments when paintings, poetry, literature and music have altered and enriched my perception of the landscape around me. I do not mean to write here in abstract terms, or of how, in general, the arts have educated and expanded my senses and emotions and given me pleasure, but of specific occasions when particular works of art have strongly connected me to the natural world.

Having spent my early childhood in India and then my later schooldays in Devon, when I went to Cambridge University, aged nineteen, it was the furthest north I had ever been. I overheard a member of the university mountaineering club telling someone about a fabulous place where it never really got dark and where you could read a newspaper outside at midnight. I thought he must be talking about the Arctic, but it was of Scotland that he spoke. The club was organising a fortnight there in the Easter vacation. I signed up immediately. It was my first experience both of rock-climbing and of snow and ice climbing. I was thrilled and frightened in equal parts. The mountains were asking questions of me and I was not sure I had all the answers. I felt challenged and also excited. I was still a confused teenager, searching for an identity. I sensed that I might have found it here. One of the group produced from his rucksack a battered and dog-eared copy of the collected poems of the mountaineer, Geoffrey Winthrop Young[1] One evening, with rain pattering on the tin roof of the mountain hut, I dipped into it.

> There is a region of heart's desire
> Free for the hand that wills;
> Land of the shadow and haunted spire;

Land of the silvery glacier fire,
Land of the cloud and the starry choir,
Magical land of hills;
Loud with the crying of winds and streams,
Thronged with the fancies and fears of dreams.

All that the wanderer's heart can crave,
Life lived thrice for its lending,
Hermit's vigil in dreamlit cave,
Dreams of the vision that Merlin gave,
Comrades till death, and a wind-swept grave,
Joy of the journey's ending:-
You who have climbed to the great white veil,
Heard ye the chant? Saw ye the Grail?[2]

The British landscape has inspired some of the greatest poetry ever written. Geoffrey Winthrop Young's poem may not be among the greatest, and it was inspired by the Alps rather than by British mountains, but this poem (longer than the two verses given here) made a huge impact on the impressionable youth that I then was. It presented an attitude to the mountains I had not been able to articulate but immediately recognised as being what, deep down, I felt.

Years later, now living permanently in Scotland, I lingered late on a winter snow-clad mountain in order to be up there when the sun set and the moon rose. A few days before, browsing without intent in the local library, I happened upon W H Murray's classic of mountain literature, *Mountaineering in Scotland*.[3] I was enraptured and intoxicated by his descriptions of the Scottish hills, especially of the winter scene by night.

Before us stretched vast snow-fields, shining frostily under the stars; beyond, rank upon rank of sparkling peaks. A great stillness had come upon the world. We seemed to tread air rather than crusted snow; we were light of foot;

we walked like demigods in joyous serenity… In the quiet I felt something of the limitations of personality fall away as desires were stilled; and as I died to self and became more absorbed in the hills and sky, the more their beauty entered in to me, until they seemed one with me and I with them.

Until my chance finding of *Mountaineering in Scotland*, my thoughts, when caught out in the dark, had dwelt on the dangers of the situation, on plummeting temperatures and matters of route finding and survival. Murray banished all such negative thoughts and showed me the glory and the wonder of the moonlit scene. Moreover he had given me permission to feel, without embarrassment, the spiritual and mystical power of the mountains at night. Now I wanted to experience for myself 'the joys of dwelling for a space on snow-fields close to the sky, where the dawn and the sunset come like armadas in slow and solemn grace, and the very air has a beauty, which we call purity.' And that night I did. Since then I have walked the mountains by moonlight and starlight many a time, but that early experience, that dawning of a new way of seeing and responding, was special.

Some years ago I hiked the trail from the rim of the Grand Canyon in Arizona down to the very bottom of it and back up again. I took more than a hundred photographs. None of them captured the effect that the canyon had on me, the awe and breathtaking astonishment. A week later I was in Washington, looking at an exhibition of nineteenth-century landscape painting. One of the works on display was of the Grand Canyon by Thomas Moran.[4] It wasn't an accurate record: colours, scale and lines were subtly altered, but here on canvas was an emotional response to the canyon similar to mine which went beyond the outward appearance to touch upon something sublime. It more accurately portrayed the canyon as a felt experience than could any of my factually correct photographs. Then, while in Ottawa on my way to Greenland, I saw an exhibition of the Canadian painter Lawren Harris whose main landscape period was from 1918-1930. His perception and interpretation of the Arctic landscape immensely enriched the way I looked at it. He was one of the Group of Seven who set out to find a style of painting which was uniquely Canadian and which would express the spirit of their land, the power of the landscape and the vastness of the North. Lawren Harris helped me appreciate the remote and monumental silence of the fjords and mountains around me, the Arctic's deep space and the beauty to be found in its minimalist elements of water, ice, rock, cloud and fog. He showed me the underlying geometry of the mountains, their simple, essential lines and curves; and ephemeral cloudscapes on broad-winged breezes in perpetual harmony with the white-robed land.

The failure of my photographs to capture the spirit of the Grand Canyon was not so much due to the shortcomings of the medium of photography as to the shortcomings of my equipment and my skill with a camera. A walking holiday in Yosemite National Park was immeasurably enriched by purchasing on arrival a copy of The Portfolios of Ansel Adams.[5] Included in this beautifully produced book was his Yosemite portfolio. Looking at his black and white photographs was a masterclass for me in the art of seeing, in finding the unusual in the usual, in being surprised by the ordinary and in discovering the familiar to be unfamiliar as if seeing it for the first time. Ansel Adams freed my eyes of conventional expectations, he taught me about Yosemite's infinite qualities of light and luminosity, about finding the quintessence of natural objects and nature's hidden patterns. His images were a meditation upon the littleness and briefness of man compared to the earth he inhabits. Ansel Adams helped me realise what it means to have a lifelong love affair with a place and its rocks, trees, clouds, rivers and lakes.

One summer my friends and I paddled from Mull's west coast out to the island of Staffa. As we approached Fingal's

Cave a tourist boat was just departing, leaving us with the cave to ourselves, amongst its high basalt columns. We explored the cave's dark depths, thrilled by the booming, echoing swell like the bass notes of a mighty cathedral organ. Emerging into the light again we pointed our bows westwards and headed for Iona. We had not gone far when we caught up with the tourist boat whose engine had broken down. Several of the men amongst the passengers had been handed oars. They raised a brave cheer as we passed them. Somebody on board had a cassette player which sent the strains of Mendelssohn's *Fingal's Cave Overture* drifting across the water. It recreated for us the essence of that cave, reinforcing what had been a mind-expanding experience – the echoing vault, the crashing surf, the brooding menace of the ocean like a sleeping monster, the high notes like light filtering through cracks into the gloom. Whenever I think of our venture into Fingal's cave, I think not only of the natural music of the sea but also of Mendelssohn music, the two mingling in my mind to create something that will stay with me forever.

When I was seven my father was posted to the North West Frontier Province of India[6] and the family moved with him. My mother occasionally took me with her to browse in the bazaars of Peshawar – a place where no British women or children were allowed without an armed male escort, for Peshawar was the 'city of a thousand and one sins,' the gateway city to the Khyber Pass. Tall, fierce Pathans in sheepskin coats swaggered about armed to the teeth. In the teeming streets were medicine-men, conjurors and snake-charmers and exotic-looking traders who had come through the mountain passes to the north from Central Asia, bringing silks from China and samovars from Russia. Lopsided carved wooden houses tottered upwards for three or four stories. There was the Street of the Storytellers and other narrow, winding lanes selling Persian lacquered bed-posts, shawls from neighbouring Kashmir, tribal jewellery, intricate gold-work, red rugs from Bokhara and embroidered thigh-length felt boots from Gilgit. And there was a little back-street shop where a wrinkled, wispy-bearded Chinese man unrolled for my mother ink-wash paintings on rice-paper or silk.[7] She bought two and gave one of them to me – an imaginary misty waterscape in subtle shades of grey, with writhing rock outcrops and vague, befogged landforms. For the next twenty-five years I looked at that painting almost every day, its spirit gradually seeping into me. Then I transferred it to my work-place, where one weekend there was a fire in my office and the painting was destroyed. Another ten years on finds me sitting in my kayak on a still day in Shetland, sea and sky merging into a single watery element. I float between mist shrouded islands, hinted headlands and stacks whose outlines are softened by moist, diaphanous veils, The sensation of being inside my lost painting is overwhelming, Drifting through this dreamscape, a Chinese artist, a Buddhist, whose name I never knew, reaches out to me across the centuries, heightening my sensitivity to nuances of tone and transparency. 'Be one with the spirit of this place,' he says. 'Become part of it and let it enter you.'

I cannot end an essay on how the arts have connected me to nature and broadened my appreciation of it without mentioning Gerard Manley Hopkins.[8] I seldom walk in the countryside without some line of his running through my head, sharpening my enjoyment – lines such as:

Glory be to God for dappled things –
For skies of couple-colour as a brinded cow:
For rose-moles all in stipple upon trout that swim;
Fresh firecoal, chestnut-falls; finches' wings;
Landscape plotted and pieced – fold, fallow, and plough;
And all trades, their gear and tackle and trim.[9]

What makes a creative work worthy of being called 'great'

is a matter for endless debate and opinions vary from one person to another. Some of the ingredients of greatness which call to me personally are that it reaches parts of me normally out of reach and moves me in ways that nothing else can. It expands my vision of the world and pushes against the frontiers of the unknowable. In the words of Christopher Fry.[10] it is 'man exploring his own amazement.' There are certain works of art – and I use the word 'art' in its widest sense – which make me feel born again. They give me the fresh vision of a child. The Gospels of *The New Testament* record the words of Jesus: 'Except a man be born again he cannot see the Kingdom of God;' and 'Except ye become as little children ye shall not enter the kingdom of Heaven.' These words can and have been interpreted as meaning that, if there is a Heaven on Earth, it is only accessible to those who retain their basic innocence, who can still see the world as if it were fresh and new and vibrant and for whom a sense of awe and wonder has not faded with the passing years. From an ancient Greek story comes the saying, 'whom the gods love die young.' My own personal interpretation of this is that the gods love those who are still young at heart when they die and who retained until the end a sense of excitement and astonishment at the beauty of the world. In helping us move towards such a state of being, great art of all kinds has a part to play.

NOTES

1 Geoffrey Winthrop Young (1876–958) was a British climber, poet and educator, and author of several notable books on mountaineering. He studied Classics at Cambridge and won the Chancellor's Medal for English Verse two years running. During the Edwardian Period, and up until the outbreak of World War I, Young made several new and difficult ascents in the Alps and also put up new routes on the crags of the Lake District and Wales. During the war, Young was at first a correspondent for the liberal *Daily News*, but later, as a conscientious objector, was active in the

Friends' Ambulance Unit. He received several decorations, but on 31 August 1917 an explosion caused injuries requiring the amputation of one of his legs. After the amputation, Young walked sixteen miles in two days to avoid being captured by the Austrians. He continued alpine climbing for a number of years – using a specially designed artificial leg that accepted a number of attachments for snow and rock work – and climbed the Matterhorn in 1928.

2 The title of this poem is 'Knight-Errantry'. It has ten stanzas in all.

3 *Mountaineering in Scotland* was written while Murray was a prisoner-of-war in Europe. It was published in 1947.

4 Thomas Moran (1837–1926). During the late 1860s, he was appointed the chief illustrator for *Scribner's Magazine*, a position that helped him launch his career as one of the premier painters of the American landscape.

5 Ansel Adams (1902–1984) was an American photographer and environmentalist. His black-and-white landscape photographs of the American West, especially Yosemite National Park, have been widely reproduced on calendars, posters, and in books. He began a career as a concert pianist but gave it up for photography. Adams used large-format cameras to ensure sharp images.

6. This is now in Pakistan, but in the 1940s, before independence and partition, it was part of India.

7. Chinese ink and wash painting, referred to as shui-mo-hua, uses only black ink, with washes of varying density. This style was developed during the Tang Dynasty (619-907).

8. Gerard Manley Hopkins (1844–1889) was an English poet, Roman Catholic convert, and Jesuit priest, whose posthumous fame established him among the leading Victorian poets. He read classics at Oxford, then, after ordination, taught in various Roman Catholic colleges and schools in England before accepting a post as Professor of Greek at Dublin University. At Oxford he developed a lifelong friendship with Robert Bridges (who became Poet Laureate) who was of importance in his development as a poet, and his posthumous acclaim. His experiments with sprung rhythm and his use of imagery

established him as a daring innovator in a period of largely traditional verse.

9 The title of this poem is 'Pied Beauty', written in 1877, but not published until 1918. Shown here are the first two stanzas.

10 Christopher Fry (1907–2005) was an English poet and playwright. He is best known for his verse dramas, notably *The Lady's Not for Burning*, which made him a major force in theatre in the 1940s and 1950s.

REINTEGRATION

The beach beyond my garden is mostly rock, seaweed, builders' rubble and amazement.

    at nature's margins
    zones where land and sea abut
    wonders never cease!

Bricks scatter the beach in various stages of erosion. Some still bear the name of brick-kilns closed long ago; others have become pink pebbles. Curving sections of brown, salt-glazed drains gradually disintegrate.

    those holes in a brick
    they brim with aquatic life
    each its own small world

  An old sandstone wall, pitted by salt winds, scarred by gale force waves and the frosts of 175 winters, defends this storm-prone town. My fingers explore uneven, abrasive surfaces, Braille-like messages eloquent to my hands. The lichen-covered wall is a feast of whites, greys and yellows, their shapes food for the imagination – archipelagos, mythical lands, abstract paintings, hyroglyphics from the Lost Continent, signals from outer space.

    crumbling old sea wall
    In a range of honey hues
    slowly returns home

  Today I find smoothed pieces of blue-white willow pattern

china lying among exactly matching mussel shells. I pick up worn and rounded sea glass – opalescent sea-gems in bottle greens, blues, jade and amber, or almost clear, all slightly frosted. Once man-made objects, they have been claimed by nature and transformed.

Mermaids' tender tears
tumbled tide-gifted jewels
ocean's offering

MORNING TIDE IN A LONELY BAY

Waves gently wash a wind-roughed beach,
Bathe bare strands in liquid opal moons,
Caress and kiss parched pebbles which
Sparkle at the tide's awakening touch.

But soon the restless, ever-changing sea,
Summoned by forces far beyond its reach,
Withdraws, exposing crab-infested reefs
And yearning sand waiting with arms outstretched.

A MENU OF MEMORIES

This is not quite 'My Life on a Plate' because it focuses mostly, but not exclusively, on unusual or bizarre meals consumed in the great outdoors. Nor is it the adventures of a gastronaut who boldly eats what no person has eaten before. It is what it is. Taste it and see.

THE MENU
A choice from:

Soup:
Sopa de Gamines
Seashore Soup

Fish:
Guddled Trout
Grackled Mackerel

Main Course:
Annapurna Dahl
Soused Welly Boots
Burned &Raw Sausages

Sweets & Puddings:
Banana Fluff & Squashed Matron's Leg

Drinks:
Mummery's Blood
A Cup of Kindness
Kagera Wedding Hooch
Whisky Wild

This menu comes from the kitchens of those two famous chefs, Messrs H Unger and F R Eshair

Head Chef's Expositions For Your Delectation

Sopa de Gamines: In 1986 I spent five weeks in Bogota, Colombia, living on the street[1] with a gang of boys.[2] These children, known as *los gamines*, had either run away from abusive, violent homes or from the appalling conditions in the sweat shops to which their parents had sold them. They survived by 'the snatch' (earrings, watches, handbags, etc), by recycling glass from the rubbish dump, begging, and by plundering hotel waste-bins. Indeed, many of the fights between gangs were about who owned the rights to which bins. From them we retrieved fish heads, chicken carcasses, bones of all sorts (with a bit of meat or gravy still clinging to them, if we were lucky), apple cores, cheese rinds, bacon rinds, potato peelings, banana skins, cabbage stalks (very edible when thinly sliced). The day's haul was either made into a massive fry-up, or turned into soup. Food was cooked over an old oil-drum containing sand soaked in petrol (siphoned off from parked cars). For mugs or bowls they used empty baked bean cans. Hunger was never far away, but what these boys were really starved of was love.

Seashore Soup: Some years ago, I decided to camp for a week on a remote part of the Scottish west coast without taking any food with me. I was interested to see if it was possible to live entirely off what I could catch or collect.[3] Seashores, I knew, were easier places than most to find food. The main ingredients of my Seashore Soup were: mussels collected from the low tide rocks, common clams and razor clams dug from recently exposed sand. There were limpets aplenty, but I never got that desperate – they taste (so I'm told) like pencil rubbers smeared with rotting fish. Cooking instructions: On a drift-wood fire (OK, I cheated and brought some matches with me), bring a pot of water to the boil and add a cloth bag containing Carragheen (a small, reddish, bushy seaweed). This exudes a gelatinous substance which thickens the soup and gives it a bit of body. Steam the shells until they open up and then scoop out the flesh, cut into smaller pieces and put into the pot. Throw in a handful of the pink and red flowers of Wild Thyme. John Right in his book, *The Edible Seashore*, says, 'forage by the sea and you can eat like a king.' All his recipes, however, involve extras such as white wine, olive oil, garlic, onions, butter and lemon juice. I had none of these things. I ate like a pauper, but a happy one because there is great satisfaction in getting back to basics.

Guddled Trout: My self-imposed survival diet included trout from the burn beside my tent. They are found by poking under the rocks and overhangs where they lurk. When one darts out, watch carefully where it goes. Slowly slide a hand into the trout's new hiding place until you feel its underside. Then tickle gently with your finger-tips. This puts the trout into some kind of trance so that it rolls into your hand and lies there. My favourite method of cooking the guddled or tickled trout was to encase it in clayish mud (there was a band of it at the back of the beach) and bury it in the hot ashes of the fire. Serve the trout with lightly boiled nettles, which are similar to spinach in texture and taste. I found that living the life of a hunter-gatherer was a full-time occupation. It took all day to forage, catch fish, collect firewood, prepare and cook the food. It was fun for a week, but a week was long enough and I was developing a terrible craving for sweet things, especially chocolate. The experience gave me a renewed appreciation of the Farmfoods store opposite my house.

Grackled Mackerel: One summer holidays, when I was sixteen, with my father and his friend, Rex, I sailed from Dartmouth across the Channel to Cherbourg on the Normandy coast. We were in my father's small cabin cruiser, *Grackle*, a sloop (a single-masted sailing boat, with a jib). It was six in the morning and I was nearing the end of my watch, while the other two slept below. *Grackle* was on a long starboard tack in a moderate wind, butting into waves of middling height. Dawn was coming up as I kept a lookout for any shipping crossing our path while steering the boat with one eye on the luminous compass and the other on the trim of the sails. I had been trailing a spinner over the stern for the last hour and half with no result when the line began to twitch and jump. *Grackle* was sailing through a shoal of mackerel. In the space of three minutes I hauled in six mackerel. I shouted through the hatch to the skipper (Dad) and Rex to get the stove going and the pan out. In less than a quarter of an hour from the last fish hitting the deck, we had gutted them, fried them in butter, and were eating them on hunks of brown bread. I had never before tasted fish as fresh as this, or so delicious. Just as wonderful was the taste of being treated as an equal by two adults and trusted to steer *Grackle* through the dark pre-dawn hours.

Annapurna Dahl: When I was 65 I had a quadruple coronary by-pass operation three months before I was due to attend a conference in Kathmandu, Nepal. On the far side of anxiety and discomfort, calling to me, were the Himalayas. They helped me through the weeks of recovery. Operation or not, there was no way I was going to be in Nepal and not go trekking. It motivated me to work hard at regaining full fitness. On arrival at Kathmandu Airport I chose, at random, a taxi driver from the jostling throng touting for my custom. Instead of taking me to my hotel, he stopped at a small tourist agency which hired out mountain guides. 'Why not?' I thought. I had made no definite plans and it would be foolish to go trekking on my own only three months after the operation. I was assigned a slim, fresh-faced young man by the name of Krishna.[4] Despite the fact that his English was limited and my Nepalese non-existent, we got on well. Our aim was, by slow degrees, to walk to a point a little short of the Annapurna Base Camp.[5] At first I thought I was looking at clouds, piling up and up. Then I realised I was seeing the High Himalayas, still miles away. A strong memory is of how we once toiled up flights of steps all day long – steps linking terraced fields and villages, one above the other, up and down which laden donkeys, as well as villagers, travelled. I recall narrow paths overarched by rhododendron as tall as trees, which carpeted the paths with their red and purple petals. Krishna was employed by a low budget agency which was not aiming at rich Europeans who expected five star meals. Every day, breakfast, lunch and supper consisted of the Nepalese national dish, dahl curry, served with plain boiled rice and sometimes a few pickled vegetables. The daily fare emerged from the backs of little mud huts in the middle of nowhere that had only a nodding acquaintance with modern hygiene. I reckoned that, as long as the food was thoroughly cooked and came direct from the pot, the risk was not too great.[6] It was filling and wholesome, and exercise and fresh air gave me a huge appetite. Now, I have only to smell lentils cooking to see again in my mind's eye those majestic peaks and to recapture that surge of joy at being granted a new lease of life.

Soused Welly Boots: In the Nuuk Fjords of West Greenland our kayak group stopped at a small fishing community and traded some surplus coffee for squares of Minke whale blubber.

Greenland is entitled to catch 211 whales, mostly common Minke whales, under a practice known as aboriginal subsistence whaling. This bypasses the 1986 ban on whaling[7] and allows whaling by communities that have traditionally relied upon whale meat in their diet. The Greenlanders, I learned, wanted to increase their quota and didn't understand how such laws could be made by people in far away cities. A Greenlandic hunter is reported as saying in some bewilderment, 'a lady in Paris says we should be vegetarian.' Usually I would have a lot of reservations about eating whale meat. Here, however, where it is embedded in the culture and where hunting methods are closer to their traditional ways than to the tactics of mass slaughter adopted by modern whaling ships, I felt no qualms about it. I was handed a piece of blubber the size of the top joint of my thumb. I chewed on it all day and it still continued to give out its rich oil – very sustaining, no doubt, but definitely an acquired taste. 'Like welly boots soaked in petrol' was how one of our group described it.

Burned & Raw Sausages: Between the ages of six and ten I was at a boarding school in the Nilgiri Hills of southern India. The school was surrounded by miles of natural forest and jungle. I am not sure whether it was the result of an enlightened belief in learning through play, or whether it was simply to give the staff a rest, but on Saturday mornings we were issued with raw rations and a box of matches and told not to come back until bedtime. My gang never did get the hang of cooking sausages over an open fire. Invariably they were burned black on the outside and almost raw on the inside. We wouldn't have wanted them any other way, for they were spiced with adventure and had the flavour of freedom.

Banana Fluff & Squashed Matron's Leg: At this same school, midnight feasts in the dormitory were always anticipated with great excitement. It took about a week to accumulate enough food, slipping it into our pockets while eating in the dining hall, and hiding it till the appointed night. When the time came to lay out the feast by torchlight in the centre of the pyjama-clad circle, the contributions were a sorry mess: squashed, covered in pocket fluff, inextricably integrated with sundry offerings which had once adhered to the handkerchief in which they had been surreptitiously wrapped, conglomerated into unlikely combinations, or sprouting interesting varieties of mould. Nonetheless, we gobbled it with delight, for it had the savour of secrecy and forbidden fruits taste the sweetest. Moreover, we were participating in a time-honoured ritual. Chief among the delights were morsels of a whitish suety roll, spotted with currants. In the dining hall, each table received a roll about two feet long. Matron's leg, we called it. Matron, she who patrolled the dormitories at night on rubber-soled shoes, was enemy number one when it came to midnight feasts. Someone was appointed as lookout. On the whispered cry of 'Cave!'[8] there would be a scramble to get back to our beds and hide the food under the covers. We were invariably caught because, next morning, there was no hiding jam stains on the sheets or pieces of Matron's leg sticking to a pillow-case.[9]

Mummery's Blood: Many admirers of W H Murray's classic of mountain literature, *Mountaineering in Scotland*, will have tried for themselves Mummery's Blood[10], Murray's famous concoction for reviving flagging climbers. 'This mountain elixir consists of equal parts of navy rum and Bovril served boiling hot. Its effect on both mind and body is nourishing, warming, strengthening; it lowers angles, shortens distances, and improves the weather.' I can vouch for that and add that it also smoothes rough waters and makes midges disappear.

A Cup of Kindness: Once, when I was in my twenties, I was hiking through North Wales. I had a heavy pack on my back and it was pouring with rain. I was weary and there were still miles to go until the next Youth Hostel. I sat down at the side of the country lane, my back to a stone wall which marked the end of a cottage garden. A white-haired woman in a flowery apron came out of the cottage and handed me a tray with a pot of tea, a mug and a large slice of cherry cake. It wasn't just the hot tea and the cake that made the remaining miles speed by, it was the kindness.

Kagera Wedding Hooch: When I reached Dar es Salaam, Tanzania's largest city, people said: 'If this seems like a backward dump, just wait till you get to Bukoba.' When I arrived in Bukoba on the western shores of Lake Victoria, the main town for Kagera Region, people said: 'if this seems like a backward dump, just wait till you get to the small villages in the bush.' Actually, 'backward dump' was far from how I see anywhere in Tanzania. There was a spontaneity and zest for life in the people I met which made me think that we, in the West, had lost something precious that they still had. I duly found myself in a small village in the outback of Kagera Region, at a wedding. One of the teachers on the course I was running had taken me along. This was a traditional tribal wedding. Men mostly wore a kunzu (an embroidered ankle-length robe) and the women a kanga (brightly printed cotton fabric wrapped around the body). Proceedings kicked off with the bride's relatives dancing to the beat of the drummers, singing about all the faults of the bridegroom and his family; then the situation was reversed, all taken in good part with much laughter. A gourd filled with village-distilled hooch made from fermented corn began to do the rounds, the guests drinking straight from the gourd. It was passed to me. I knew people were watching to see how this white stranger would react. Now it so happened that, at that time, one in three persons in the region was HIV positive. Indeed, one theory was that the AIDS epidemic had started here and spread to the rest of the world. In these circumstances, exchanging body fluids was extremely dangerous. The rim of the gourd had been touched by many lips and was wet with saliva. Not to drink would cause great offence. What should I do? What would you have done?

Whisky Wild: I was in my second year of kayaking and with a group of four other similarly inexperienced paddlers. We found ourselves on an exposed stretch of sea with the wind rising and the waves growing bigger by the minute. To return to base we would have to paddle with the wind on our backs.

That is to say, with the curling, breaking waves coming up unseen behind us before charging on ahead – always the most scary kind of paddling. And we were scared, no doubt about it. We formed a raft by laying our paddles across our decks so that they overlapped and tucking them tight into our bodies with our elbows. Someone produced a hip-flask of whisky and passed it along the line. The waves hurled our raft forward, no paddling required, while we downed the whisky and sang at the tops of our voices, *To Be a Wild Rover*, competing with the roar of the sea, thumping the decks in time to the tune, keeping fear at bay.

> I've been a wild rover for many a year
> And I spent all my money on whiskey and beer,
> And now I'm returning with gold in great store
> And I never will play the wild rover no more.
> (Thump,thump, thump, THUMP!)
>
> *chorus:*
> And it's no, nay, never,
> (Thump, thump, thump, THUMP!)
> No nay never no more,
> Will I play the wild rover
> No never no more.
> (Thump, thump, thump, THUMP!)

In fact, the adrenalin rush of this roller-coaster ride whetted our appetites for more and wilder roving.

NOTES

1 My book, *Fallen Angels* (Canongate, 1992) resulted from this experience.

2 There were about a dozen boys in the gang, ranging in age from 8-13. Since then, a more enlightened administration in Bogota´ has

made the city a safer place and also started more programmes to help the street children. Worldwide, the number of children living on the street continues to rise and is currently thought to be over 100 million.

3 If you are tempted to try something similar, bear in mind that laws abound regarding what you can collect and where you can collect it – by-laws about conservation, trespass, the right to roam, etc. They vary from one place to another. Research is needed before you do anything like this. Also, do not eat shellfish of any sort in areas where the water is polluted.

4 I realised that Krishna would never progress as a guide unless his English improved. I managed to get a place for him on a British Council course in Kathmandu. He now owns his own Himalayan Guide company.

5 Annapurna (25,545 ft) was first climbed by a French expedition in 1950.

6 This proved to be the case, but, when I then went to the five-star hotel in Kathmandu for the conference, I relaxed my guard and ate a salad – and paid the penalty.

7 Commercial whaling was banned in 1986 by the International Whaling Commission (IWC), the body responsible for managing whaling. The IWC regulates the whaling industry and acts to conserve whale populations. The ban was introduced because some species were in danger of being wiped out. The IWC has nearly 90 member countries, including the UK. But three member nations – Norway, Iceland and Japan – have lodged objections to the ban and continue to whale commercially.

8 Latin for 'Beware'. Pronounced 'KV' (by we schoolboys, anyway).

9 Should readers form the impression from these two items that boarding school was all wizard fun and jolly japes, let me say that I think sending young children away from their homes and their parents can be emotionally very damaging. I am not in favour of boarding schools and did not send my own children to any such institutions.

10 Albert Frederick Mummery was a Victorian mountaineer and author whom Murray greatly admired both for his pioneering climbs in the Alps and the quality of his writing about these exploits.

RIVER

High summer. Dappled by sunlight through forest foliage, River is in spate after heavy rain, its peat-brown water churning white, falling, falling to the distant sea. Flung against boulders, blocks and angles, bouncing off the bottom, cascading over sills and ledges, with thunderous forces in collision, River is in full voice. Boiling cauldrons, bursting blisters, chutes, jets and spouts, upwellings, swellings, swirls and sudden holes, crests and troughs and standing waves, smooth dark tongues, reverse eddies, riffling shallows, cataracts and rapids all rushing, roiling, gushing, splashing, plunging, dancing, sliding, falling, falling towards the sea. And yet... River is a paradox – in its continually repeated shapes and forms, motionless motion, unchanging change.

Burns leap down hillsides, hurtle through ravines or glide through the leaf-floored forest to pay their tribute. Each burn is fed by rivulets and runnels of ever-decreasing size, and these by tiny trickles and microscopic pores that drain the soil. River is a complex system penetrating the land for miles around, its length infinite and incalculable.

Landscape sculptor, creator of glens and gorges, excavator of the Earth's bare bones, River is the sun's energy, the voice of gravity. Falling, falling towards the sea, River is nature out of balance, disorder seeking order, the absolute imperative for equilibrium.

River is older than the flow of human blood in human veins. Our early ancestors stared into its dark depths and felt its mystery. Like thoughts flowing through the mind, River was sometimes troubled, sometimes serene, sometimes uncontrollable, the abode of slippery eels and fish which rose unbidden to the surface. River was the unnamed fear that lies around the bend. Peat-stained and silt-heavy, River was a woman's menstrual flow. Reflected in River were the sky, the clouds and the sun. When our ancestors drank its water they drank the firmament above. River was the means of survival and a frequent cause of death, benign, malicious, unpredictable, a natural force to be appeased. And River told of life's journey from birth, through vigorous youth and sedate old age to final union with the ocean where all rivers become one. Rich with powerful symbols embedded in the human psyche, River runs through our subconscious minds and our dreams.

Stone Age hunter-gatherers had an intimacy with River that few of us now have. They picked berries on these banks and set traps for fish. They shared River with brown bears, wolves, otters, elk, wild boar and lynx. They knew River's different tastes, smells and sounds, and the feel of it beneath their bare feet. They experienced River in all its moods, in all seasons, all weathers, all conditions. They were there when drought exposed gravel bars and water-rounded rock and the sun winked from shrinking pools. They knew both River's wrath and its tranquil moods when ripples and bubbles dropped shadows on time-smoothed slabs. By night they saw silvered pebbles and pools of liquid moon. They observed the autumn leaves, under rainbow skies, choking the flow, making dams and lakes. In winter's iron-hard grip, with River silent and bound fast by ice, were long icicles where waterfalls had been and shattered ice in splinter-patterns of wondrous design. And they rejoiced as reawakening water gurgled and murmured beneath the ice, heralding the advent of spring.

These men and women, so close to the rhythms of the land, with their mythic and poetic minds, heard River's voice shouting, chuckling, sobbing, roaring, making prophecies, suggesting stories: Salmon, a hero figure on a quest, who answered the call that cannot be denied, entering a new and strange world with many a twist and obstacle along the way – a story that ends with the hero's return and his death. Reeds whispered the secrets of the gods and in spiralling whirlpools was the inward winding labyrinth at whose centre the answer to the riddle might be found.

River is a song with natural harmonies – the flecked bark of a silver birch and the white-streaked race; bubbles conglomerating in a bay and a dragonfly's compound eye; the writhing fibres of an old, bare log bobbing beneath grained granite walls; red berries dangling over the spot where salmon will conceal their eggs; a drifting feather, the feathering on forming ice; crystal streams dropping over quartz-veined cliffs; a limb of oak reaching out from the river bank – a river of time, each ring a year of growth. River is structured like a tree, widest at the base, tapering upwards, branching and branching again into ever smaller fractals of itself. Bucking river waves, light waves and sound waves, the shock waves from an earthquake – all have the same properties, obey the same laws; coiled foam on black, still pools and the whirling galaxies of outer space.

Cycles of birth and death are enacted on every scale. Water insects with a lifespan of a day flit in the shade of a willow that has sheltered ten thousand generations of their kind. The cycle of the seasons, our planet's precious moisture in constant circulation;and, measured in millennia, the repeated rise and erosion of mountain ranges. Falling, falling to the sea, River keeps time to the heartbeat of the universe.

MAGICAL SEA CAVES & MINOTAURS' LAIRS

Caves can be compelling and powerful places. They are the entrance to the Underworld. They can arouse thoughts about hidden treasure, secret things, pirates, smuggling, cellars, dungeons, gnomes and trolls; about penetrating to the heart of things, or the suppressed, dark emotions of the subconscious, or about hermits deeply meditating. Caves have been equated to the womb, and entering or exiting them to procreation and birth. Shamans, when going into a trance or reaching a state of ecstasy, liken it to falling down a long, dark tunnel before suddenly emerging into bright light and new and strange world. People who have had near-death experiences describe them in much the same way. (One wonders what prompted Lewis Carroll to write of Alice falling down a seemingly bottomless rabbit hole to emerge in Wonderland). The psychology of caves is complex and full of opposites: enfolding security and being held closely and lovingly, or feelings of suffocation and claustrophobia; the urge to explore and see what lies around the corner, or fear of the dark, of the unknown, of unseen dangers; the maze as entrapment, or as a means of liberation through finding the centre. Often we feel these opposites, these co-existing contraries tugging inside us.

Mackinnon's cave on Staffa was my introduction to sea caves. It is bigger, but less accessible and less well-known than Fingal's Cave on the same island. We heard the cave before we saw it – a hollow panting like a wounded Minotaur crouching somewhere in its depths. The swell funnelled into the cave with a roar, only to swash out again minutes later. We hovered close to the dark, gaping mouth, back-paddling so as not to be swept in out of control, manoeuvring our kayaks, waiting for the right moment, sorting ourselves into single file.

Between the churning chaos of the outgoing water and the roaring surge of the next incoming swell was a moment of calm.

'Now!' I shouted.

As we entered the cave there was a flurry of wings overhead. Half a dozen alarmed puffins zoomed out. Every drip from the vaulted ceiling, every sucking and gurgling was magnified into booming echoes. The next swell swept in, blotting out the light from the entrance. Higher and higher rose our kayaks as the wave filled the cave. I could feel the pressure in my ears as the air compressed. Then I was battling to prevent myself being washed out again as water cascaded from ledges and the cave half emptied. Our exclamations – a mixture of awe and alarm – reverberated around the high chamber. We moved forward in the dim light, making use of the calm intervals and trying to hold our own during the bits when it seemed all Hell had broken loose. At the far end of the outer chamber the cave roof was much lower. Up we rose again as another swell flooded in. I was sure my head was going to bang against the rocky roof. I flattened myself along the deck, feeling my back press against the rock ceiling. Only about a foot of air-space was left. The increasing air pressure was becoming painful to the ears. Then the wave fell away, sloshing and swirling out of the cave.

Nowhere in the British Isles has sea caves in quite such abundance or as large and labyrinthine as the Shetlands. The biggest cave in Britain – bigger than the caves in Cheddar Gorge – is a sea cave north of St Magnus Bay on the mainland of Shetland, which is 60ft tall and spanning a floor area of 5,600 square metres. My introduction to Shetland's sea caves was on Mousa, an island off the southern eastern end of Mainland Shetland – caves full of treasure: shoals of tiny translucent fish; a luminous viridian pool illuminated by a shaft of light where the cave roof had partly collapsed; pink sea anemones on red rock; blow holes through which the swell snorted and escaped in explosive gusts; a booming drum-beat which turned out to be the surf pounding the beach of a connected cave. In one cave we managed to scrape through the eye of a needle at the far end into another cave, finally emerging about two hundred yards further along the coast. Most of the caves were long and narrow, forcing us to ship our paddles, there being no room to wield them, and to propel ourselves forward by pushing against the walls with our hands. Occasionally the walls would move further apart, leaving us groping for support, leaning out of balance. A swell kept sweeping in, sluicing along the walls. Not surprisingly, one of us capsized. In the restricted space, in semi-darkness, with kayaks and paddles banging against each other, against the walls and against the low roof, our rescue drill was not exactly a model of efficiency.

On the western side of the island of Yell we explored a sea cave whose entrance was protected by a huge waterfall tumbling from the cliffs above. A narrow gap between the roaring, downward hurtling water and the cave's limpet-encrusted portals enabled us to creep into the gloomy interior. Seen from the inside, this liquid, flickering, translucent curtain held us spellbound. We moved to far end of the main chamber, then bumped and scraped round a corner into complete darkness. We decided that, just for a few minutes, we would not turn on our head-torches. I had never met total and absolute darkness before. It was a tangible, unnerving presence. The fear of losing contact with the others was strong. We kept calling to each other. Someone's bows crashed into me. Normally I might have felt slightly annoyed. That day I was mightily comforted and reassured. From the echoes I guessed this was a smaller, narrower chamber. Being cut off from the force of the swell, it was calmer. Afraid of bumping my head I inched cautiously into the blackness, keeping one wall within touching distance of my paddle. The magnified hissing breath of my companions, loud drippings and the water sobbing in cracks and fissures eerily filled the darkness. Someone snapped on his head-torch and we all followed suit, glad the experience was over. With senses heightened by tension and eyes grateful for the light, we gazed at the blackly gleaming, quartz-streaked architecture of blocks, slabs, pillars and angled walls. Somewhere above us small ponies were grazing and corn rippling in the wind, but here we were in another world, a magical and very different world.

REFLECTIONS ON A MISTY LOCH

Ambivalent sea and sky,
Imperceptible qualities of grey,
And I, more reflection than reality,
Merge in silvered glass, the future with the past;
And dreaming fluid, limbo dreams,
Slide through shoals of waning suns,
Intangible elisions which magnify, extend,
Till rain moon-craters the mirrors of my mind.

WOLF

Burial mounds, graveyards, a war memorial and a monument all mark Strath Kildonan's dead and departed. A wolf is remembered here too. The last wolf in Sutherland. The words on the stone leave room for rejoicing and for regret. Regret, because we recognize Wolf in ourselves. Our ancestors respected a fellow hunter, bound by the same laws – the co-operation, loyalty and obedience of the pack, its hierarchies and territorial instinct.

Wolf is present in that pull of opposites which sparks our creativity: the need for both order and chaos, for the garden and the forest, safety and danger, freedom and the ties of belonging. Wolf pads through our psyche. He is the craving for mystery, for a sense of otherness, for something elemental and beyond ourselves.

In the upper reaches of the glen, on the tower of a small stone kirk, a bell once tolled, summoning the faithful flock. The kirk serves as a monument to Wolf's demise. Inside, a leather-bound book proclaims: 'Man shall have dominion over everything that moves on this earth,' and 'shall have sovereignty over the animals.' A bleeding figure hangs from a cross, a sacrifice to atone for our sins, the ritual scapegoat who took the blame. Wolf was the focus for man's prejudice and fears, He was demonised and ruthlessly exterminated. High on a hill, long ago, a hunted wolf howled, trying in vain to gather his non-existent pack.

The crofters existed at the margins and limits of where crops could grow and livestock thrive. One poor harvest or a few cattle lost could bring them to the brink of starvation. Wolf walked the same narrow line, stared into the same abyss. Like the travelling folk in the area, Wolf lived on the fringes, an outsider. Who is welcome and who is not? Who has rights and who does not? Nature's answers are not our own.

In the natural world edge-lands are where different ecologies meet – at river banks or where the wild woods touch the moor. These are rich and varied habitats, as are borders and boundaries where ideas, races and cultures mix. Margins and edges are places of change and adventure, of great learning and great suffering.

These glens have experienced all kinds of clearances. Iron age farmers cleared the native woodland; men rid the country of bears, aurochs and wolves. Enforced by fire and by red-coated soldiery, crofters were ordered off land they had farmed for generations. Later, acres of heather were burned to improve grouse shooting; and disciplined ranks of alien, green-coated conifers were uprooted or felled for their timber. Different owners, power structures and land use will bring more clearances, ones we cannot foresee, as the old makes way for the new. Many seasonal cycles after Wolf lingered on the threshold of extinction, Highlanders stood on the shore waiting to cross an immense ocean. Echoing down the centuries are the piper's farewell lament and the last wolf's lonely cry.

Gold was discovered in this river. Men rushed to sift its shingle for the precious metal. Then new means of making money were found. These seekers after wealth paid little heed to the other gold that was there: foliage on the turn, shimmering in a low sun; the last autumn leaves floating in a pool; sunlight on sun-bleached grass; the red-gold of old bracken; golden sands and glinting ice-bound lochs; and, once upon a time, Wolf's amber eyes and his tawny coat glowing in a soft dawn light. This is the true wealth of the land.

In landscape beauty there is both unity and diversity. There is harmony on all scales from the broad sweep of the mountains to the symmetry and design of one little plant; and there is resonance between big and small, between stags' antlers and forked trees; between a wet peat bog on a starry night and the deep blue-black of a beetle's back. Wolf was completely at one with his environment, fully adapted. The beauty of the whole countryside was in him, just as he was part of it. No more does an unseen presence miraculously merge and melt into tree-bark and speckled rock. Wolf's silence is eloquent on a beauty we will never know again.

Nature is out of balance here and incomplete. Something is missing. Small colonies of exquisite plants, once the glory of this place, give evidence that Wolf no longer keeps the nibbling deer on the move. Without the top predator everything is changed, evolved patterns of dependency disrupted, Nature's checks and balances in disarray. Something is missing. Over these glens, mountains and moors lies a yearning emptiness, an aching absence that is Wolf.

In the high country where the wind blows free, the spirit of Wolf is strong. On the rolling hills which matched his undulating gait; on the ribbed and brindled mountain flanks where grey mists ghost towards grazing deer, the essence of Wolf lingers yet.

The Flow Country was a hunting ground for Wolf; the wind a river of information for keen nostrils, tongues and ears. This hummocky, tussocky expanse of seepage and soligenous flush, of moss mosaics, gleys and gullies rendered up to Wolf not only deer, but hares and birds' eggs and, in hard times, voles and frogs.

Complex patterns of bog-pools, the moor's upturned eyes, bear witness to brawling skies, migrating geese, the long northern after-glow and a thousand moons. Look hard and, in the dark peaty waters, you may catch a glimpse of Wolf. Or is it but the flicker of an ancient memory, the shadow of a dream? This landscape is a never-ending dance, a ceaseless symphony. Listen carefully and you may hear, singing with the thunder, with the bubbling burns, the swash and churn of waterfalls, with shaking branches and the softly sibilant grass, a keening voice, wild and eerie. Or is it but the sighing and sobbing of the wind?

We pacified the wilderness, deepening our alienation from nature. But, as Henry Thoreau said: 'Wildness is the preservation of the World.' Through wilderness and wildness, Wolf's wilderness and wildness, we find healing and wholeness and answers to questions we have not yet learned to ask.

Wolf is the prophet and forerunner of our fate. As we drift in the vast ocean of time, in the ebb and flow of space, the distance between Wolf's extinction and the death of Planet Earth, is infinitesimal. In a largely lifeless galaxy, and before we vanish from the Universe, we should treasure what living company we have in a spirit of co-existence and a belief in the oneness of all things.

LEAPING OFF THE CLIFF

Beyond fear's edge
Time expands
And galaxies extend, ablaze with meaning,
A universe contained within one heart-beat,
Vanishing into deep lacunae of the mind:
Elusive shadow of a swiftly passing bird,
Once glimpsed
Forever sought.

BECAUSE IT'S DAFT

W H Murray (1913–1996) wrote two of the great classics of mountain literature – *Mountaineering in Scotland* and *Undiscovered Scotland.*[1] Murray's passion for the mountain environment in all its aspects and moods radiates from every page of these two books and from his accounts of his Himalayan expeditions. In describing what drew him to mountains and mountaineering Murray puts into words what many a climber and hill-walker has felt but could not express, or did not recognise in themselves until he showed them.

On arriving at the top of his very first peak – the Cobbler, near Arrochar in Scotland – Murray writes: 'I had never dreamt that my own country held wild land so vast. I recognised on the instant that every peak had to be known,' thus neatly summarising three of his strongest motives: a love of wild, remote places, the sense of freedom they gave and the thrill of exploration. Time and again in Murray's books we see his strong impulse to rove and explore and the enthralling pleasures of discovering the undiscovered country. 'Exploratory quest on whatever plane,' he says, 'is integral to living. Man cannot opt out and remain man.'

Closely linked to a yearning for the undiscovered places is a desire for freedom – freedom from petty regulations, the urban clutter, crowds and confining city streets and from the routine and demands of everyday life. What comes over strongly in his two classics, though, is that he is not trying to get away from something negative, but is going to something positive. Life, Murray says, is seen in a more detached way and in its proper perspective when contemplated from a mountain-top. 'Were a man to achieve little else in his life he would none the less, in achieving this, possess a pearl of great price – an individual mind and the peace that is true freedom.'

Another aspect of freedom as valued by Murray is the freedom to put one's life at risk. As mountaineers do, he often chose a harder way to the top rather than an easier one because of the challenge and the risk involved. For him, risk is what raises climbing above being just a game; it gives it a special edge and meaning and, as for many a climber, life is never so sweet as when there is a possibility of losing it. This is what makes the adrenalin flow, the nerves tingle and provides that feeling of being really alive. It is clear from *Mountaineering in Scotland*, its sequel *Undiscovered Scotland* and from his quasi-autobiography, *The Evidence of Things Not Seen*, that what draws Murray to climbing on the great routes, particularly winter climbing, is the nervous tension and suspense which builds up until the top is reached. Then comes the relaxation and exhilaration. That special blend of delight and danger, he says, is the secret of the mountains.

Raising a bottle of beer and making a toast in the Western Desert to 'Mountains' with his German captor, a fellow mountaineer, he says: 'Mountains give us some good things such as friends worth having, battles worth fighting, beauty worth seeing.' In using the word 'battles' he does not mean that he regards mountains as the enemy. He means something akin to a tournament, a sporting contest, a challenge to be accepted.

There is, too, the animal physicality of the contest, 'the joy of swarming over this brow of space was out of all proportion to the technical difficultly. One's blood spins and the spirit sings. No melancholy in a man can survive such rock.' At other times there is sheer elation in facing high, bitter winds, and in the hard play of muscles. As Murray shows us, one aspect of this physicality is getting back to the basics of survival and safety, simple food, warmth and shelter and, through this, refreshing our appetite for life. Murray describes what it is like to be ensconced in the mountain hut at the foot of the Ben Nevis cliffs – the iron stove is creating a warm fug, his bunk, after the long hard walk up to the hut, seems the most comfortable bed he has ever had as he watches the stove glow red through the darkness and listens to wind thunder on the walls and roof.

Recalling his winter ascent of Tower Ridge on Nevis, fighting a gale at dusk to cross the icy gash of Tower Gap, Murray writes of 'the exhilarating contest with the elements, upon mountains that may be won, yet never conquered: shared by companions who may be defeated, yet whose spirit I have never seen shaken.'

Murray is aware of the mental challenge, too. The mental battle is not with the mountains, but with oneself – against one's own weaknesses, fears, doubts, lack of resolution and narrow perspectives. Of his winter ascent of Observatory Ridge on Ben Nevis, Murray says it was the longest and hardest climb in relation to sheer strain that he would ever do and then he goes on to say that when one stands on the summit after such a climb it is not the mountain that is conquered, 'We have conquered self and the mountain has helped us.' The appeal of the problem-solving aspect of mountaineering is obvious from Murray's descriptions of trying to work out how to surmount the seemingly insurmountable, of planning the logistics of a long expedition, finding the way through thick mist, or calculating the risks involved. There is the thrill of mind and body working in harmony, of skill and craftsmanship applied through co-ordinated limbs, trained reflexes and bodily fitness. When good form is struck, he comments, when it all comes together, you rise from the dead. The world is yours. 'Of a sudden I struck form. Eye, mind and muscle co-ordinated, and I felt myself drift up the cliffs like smoke.'

Descriptions like these show what it is like be 'in the flow' (other have called it being 'in the zone' or 'in the groove'). The psychologist, Mihaly Csikszentmihalyi, who specialised in flow theory and its connection to happiness and creativity, describes being in the flow as a state of complete concentration and absorption in which your ego falls away as your whole being becomes involved in the task; action follows upon action according to an internal logic which seems to need no conscious intervention on our part and there is little distinction between self and environment; between stimulus and response; or between past, present and future [3].

In describing his adventures Murray stresses again and again the joy of sharing them with like-minded friends. When climbing companions share danger, hardship and beauty, when they put their lives in each other's hands, it creates strong bonds, a team spirit and a sense of camaraderie. The rope that links them on the mountain becomes 'the surest bond life yields of friendship.' Mountains, Murray says, gave him lasting friendships more priceless than accumulations of gold.

Murray writes of the black bristle of the Cuillin leaping to the eye of the mountaineer as lightning to steel. He was entranced by the sheer beauty of the mountains, a beauty he had experienced in all seasons, all weathers, by day and by night. Moreover, he shows us their beauty on all scales, from the tiniest alpine flower to a vast panorama; and he is aware, and makes us aware, of the underlying unity and harmony of the natural landscape. What makes his writing so memorably able to capture the wonder of it all is that he responds to this beauty both with his senses and with his soul.

After Murray's prisoner-of-war experience and his discovery of the perennial philosophy of mysticism and meditation, his biggest single reason for mountaineering is that mountains provide not only physical exploration, but also an inner journey of self-discovery, personal development, and growth towards a oneness with the Divine, or the ultimate reality of Truth and Absolute Beauty. The undiscovered country of the mountains gave access to the undiscovered country of the mind. The lack of distinction between self and the mountains, identified by Csikszentmihalyi, is very close to achieving the 'oneness' with the Divine that Murray saw as the ultimate goal both of his life and of his mountaineering. For Murray, the way to find this unity was through an awareness and appreciation of mountain beauty, heightened and sharpened by the physical struggle and by being in the flow: 'In the quiet I felt something of the limitation of personality fall away as desires were stilled; and as I died to self and became more absorbed in the hills and sky, the more their beauty entered into me, until they seemed one with me and I with them.'

Most climbers and hill-walkers will have trembled on the brink of this kind of awareness without being able to articulate it or, perhaps, willing to admit to such feelings. Murray's honesty about his own reactions to the mountains makes it possible for new generations of climbers to appreciate the spiritual dimensions of mountaineering.

As with all enjoyable activities, part of the pleasure lies in reliving them. And like most mountain-goers, Murray had a treasure trove of memories, so that the brilliant climbs, the wonderful views, the epic adventures, the tranquil moments and the good company could be taken out and enjoyed over and over again. After relating the arduous journey to reach Nevis, the heavy loads carried to the summit and the cold, uncomfortable night spent there, he declares: 'For all this work and unpleasantness we have, say the Philistines, nothing to show except one gully climb. Nothing to clink in our pockets, so to speak. Nothing but a memory. A memory of the wide silent snow-fields crimsoned by the rioting sky, and of the frozen hills under the slow moon. These have remained with us.'

Although he expresses them so much more eloquently than most, Murray's reasons for being drawn to the mountains and to wilderness areas are much the same as those of the majority of us who seek pleasure and fulfilment in such places. However, he acknowledges the subjective and personal nature of our individual reasons but declares that there is one common factor that all mountains share without question –

enjoyment. As Murray points out, the original meaning of the Scots word 'daft' was 'crazy with happiness,' or something that put you in this state. Therefore, he maintains, mountaineers and mountaineering are daft.'

In everything that Murray writes about mountains and wilderness areas it is clear that this joy, this daftness, stems from a physical, mental, emotional and spiritual closeness and contact with the environment around him. Murray reminds us, more persuasively than most, that we are part of the wilderness and not separate from it. Climbing narratives can be put into three categories: conquest, caretaking and connection. Conquest narratives are about domination, putting flags on peaks, naming a route, national pride or earning bragging rights. Caretaking stories display sympathy for and appreciation of the natural world and concern to preserve it so that we may continue to experience it. Although not as damaging as conquest narratives, they do treat the environment as a human resource, there to be used for our convenience. In connection narratives the writer is not an outsider but part of the natural world. There is a heightened awareness of the mountains, nature and wilderness and a sense of unity and harmony with them. Murray is in this third category of writing – a category which teaches that we are part of nature and the wilderness and essential to its survival, just as it is essential to our survival. As Jay Griffiths says: 'The human mind developed in wilderness and needs it still.' In the face of mounting ecological and environmental disaster the world desperately needs writers of Murray's calibre and wisdom who can reconnect us with the natural world. He reconnects us by showing us rather than telling us, by sharing with us what made him daft. He takes us with him to the places he loves and speaks to us from the heart.

NOTES

1 Although Bill Murray died in 1996 I have used the present tense in

this essay because his two classics of mountain literature are still very much alive. Since its publication in 1947, *Mountaineering in Scotland* has never been out of print and continues to be read by and to open the eyes of each new generation of mountaineers and hill walkers.

2 A combined volume of these two books edited by Ken Wilson was published in 1979 by Diadem Books and reissued several times after that by Bâton Wicks Publications (ed. Ken Wilson).

3 Mihaly Cszikszentmihalhyi, *Flow: The Psychology of Optimal Experience* (Harper and Row, 1990)

A SENSE OF PLACE

Here are six short pieces about places which have been a part of my life. This is not an anthology of the most beautiful places I have seen – that would need a much longer list than this. They are locations I visit fairly often, either physically because they are nearby, or mentally because I was there on those occasions, which we all have in our lives, when we seem to pack a huge amount of living and intense experiences into a brief span of time. They have been selected, too, because, in all of them I have felt close to things wild and elemental.

Loch Long

Apart from the Gareloch,[1] Loch Long, which forms the eastern boundary of the Cowal Peninsular, is the nearest sea loch to me and the one I visit most often. Like many of Scotland's sea lochs it reaches far into the mountains, creating contrast and an intertwining between land and water, each displaying the other to good effect. In its waters thrive cod, whiting, plaice, mackerel, skate, wrasse, pollack, spurdog and migratory fish such as salmon and sea trout. Humans are not the only ones to enjoy the fishing, for seals and dolphins come here too. From the Firth of Clyde the loch extends in a north-easterly direction for twenty miles, varying in width between one and two miles. However, its name is not derived from its length, but from the Gaelic word 'long' for ship. The head of the loch is only a mile and a half away from inland, freshwater Loch Lomond where the village of Tarbet takes its name from 'tairbeart' meaning 'isthmus', or literally 'draw-boat'. In 1236 Viking raiders did just that, sailing down Loch Long then, using logs as rollers, hauling their boats across the land gap to Loch Lomond where they plundered the settlements along its shores.

On the eastern side of the loch is a road, an oil terminal, a sprinkling of houses and a place where nuclear warheads are loaded onto ships from the bunkers that run deep into the flanks of Glen Douglas, but the western shores have a feeling of remoteness and wildness. Mile after mile are tiny bays and headlands. There is always one more corner to see round, one more surprise: perhaps a view up a secluded glen, a secret cove or a burn tumbling into the loch. Thickly forested slopes rise steeply from the shore - a mixture of tall, dark conifers and native oak, birch and hazel. In the taller trees Herons keep watch. These shores are the habitat of sea-ducks such as the common eider, the common goldeneye and red-breasted mergansers. Sometimes the trees overhang the water and I paddle through cool cloisters, carpeted with petals or floating leaves. In other places the banks are lined with clumps of purple-flowering rhododendrons. On calm days the forest is reflected in the loch, a green line of treetops jagging through the water, with my paddle creating whorls amongst billowing clouds and swaying forest. At low tide, when are revealed submerged boulders like pale ghosts, and a multi-coloured sub-aqua seaweed jungle, the visual effects when these are overlaid by the reflections from the land are a feast for the eye.

At high tide I can paddle close to steep-sided rocks which plunge sheer into the loch. Carved slabs of schist and quartz slide into a pellucid zone, palely shining like amber, onyx, carnelian or jade. I can reach out and touch the ancient, ice-chiselled, sea-smoothed bones of the earth, every inch a marvel of grain and texture upon which dances dappled light from rippling water or swaying boughs. Over these time-etched rocks, in shades of white, yellow and grey, lichens spread their fantastic shapes. The world's finest galleries of modern art could not hold an exhibition to rival these works of nature.

One fresh spring day, seven and a half centuries after the Viking long ships came this way a slim kayak was marauding down the loch, its occupant capturing other kinds of treasure with notebook and camera. The sea rolled down the loch at a lively pace, each wave gathering under my thighs like a horse bunching for the gallop. Revelling in the motion, I sped joyously towards the purple silhouettes of Ben Vorlich, Ben Arthur and Ben Narnain while, beyond their jagged ridges, armadas of clouds sailed in from the west. The wind herding white breakers down the loch, sheep on the hillside, the curving arc of a white wing, the crescent of snow on Beinn Ime – the world was in harmony, ever-moving, ever-changing, beautiful harmony.

The Fruin Hills

The Fruin Hills are a fifteen-minute drive from my house in Helensburgh. They are not particularly spectacular or high. For the most part they are rounded, with the occasional crag or bluff, bare of trees and with tops around six and seven hundred metres (averaging about 2,000 feet). These are the hills in which I walk most frequently. I have the same fondness for them one has for an old friend. Despite their fairly humble height, the views are rewarding, sometimes astounding. To the North lie mile upon mile of mountain ranges. The eastern flanks overlook Loch Lomond. To the west are the two sea lochs of the Gareloch and Loch Long. Looking south one sees first, Glen Fruin, flat and green, with its river meandering towards Loch Lomond. Beyond that is the Clyde Estuary opening out to the sea, with a vista far down the Ayrshire coast. On a good day the granite dome of Ailsa Craig, the half-way point between Glasgow and Belfast, is visible.

Because of their proximity to my home, I can be amongst the Fruin Hills without too much delay when they call. And they call often. If Helensburgh is shrouded in mist, I grab my gear and go, for there is a good chance that the Fruin tops are poking their heads above it. It thrills me to stand on a hilltop, with a sea of cloud lapping at my feet, peaks protruding all around like little islands, feeling the sun on my face and knowing that, down there, cars are driving about with their headlights on. Or, if I wake to find there's been a hard frost overnight, I am up there an hour later, before the sun has done its work, crunching over the frost-encrusted wonderland. Because of my familiarity with these hills, descending in the dark, on tried and tested routes, holds few hazards, enabling me to stay up there to watch a sunset, or enjoy a stroll under a full moon. Similarly, to arrive on a summit when dawn is breaking is easier for me here than anywhere else. I recall a dawn one May morning when, as the glow from the North-East grew stronger, a Flamingo cloud flowed up the hillside and poured over the ridge.

The scale of the Fruins is such that it is possible to walk the entire course of any one of its burns, from where it joins the River Fruin to the point where it bubbles out of the mountainside. In the space of a couple of hours I have experienced, on a mini-scale, a tree-filled gorge, a steep gulley requiring a scramble, several waterfalls and a mile or more of tinkling burn, tumbling or wrinkling over smooth slabs. In autumn, to walk the broad-backed ridges is like being on the back of a great tawny beast, lion-coloured, or tiger-striped. When the hills are under a thin covering of snow, with dead grass and bracken showing through, the scattering of stunted trees standing like skeletons, I feel sometimes as if I am in an etching, the stark, gaunt beauty, strongly accentuated. In early spring, after the snow has left the hills but before the new growth has begun, the land is a symphony of browns: vibrant oboe umbers; deep burnt sienna bassoons; flaring brass trumpets where bleached grass is lit by the sun.

I will end with an extract from a diary I was keeping some years ago: '8th February 1998 – The rhythm of walking got my thoughts going, but every now and then I stopped and absorbed the incredible beauty – the dark reds of the old bracken and the whiteness of the adjacent snow patches; clouds dark and brooding, or radiant with the sun behind them; the sun glinting on ice; and on parts of the Firth of Clyde; wind-blown snow shifting across the ground, and snow-dunes all lined up in the same direction.'

The Endrick Water

The Endrick Water starts where two burns join, one running off the Gargunnock Hills, the other off the Fintry Hills. The result of this union flows south west into the southern end of Loch Lomond, It is the largest of the several rivers entering the loch. From its source to the shores of Loch Lomond, as the crow flies, is sixteen miles, but, due to its winding course, the actual length is double that figure. The Endrick's conservation credentials are impeccable: a Site of Special Scientific Interest, a candidate to become a Special Area of Conservation, part of the Loch Lomond and Trossachs National Park and of the Loch Lomond National Nature Reserve, and the subject of reports from The Scottish Environmental Protection Agency, RSPB and other conservation agencies. There are good reasons for this: it is a spawning river for Atlantic Salmon – they make their way to the upper reaches of the river via the Firth of Clyde, the River Leven, Loch Lomond and the Endrick itself. It is a breeding river for lampreys[2] which are becoming increasingly rare in Europe, with the black dwarf lamprey being unique to the Endrick Water. The meadowlands of the lower Endrick flood in winter providing an excellent habitat for a wide range of wildfowl. The mixed woodland along the banks and the wetlands, between them, support well over fifty species of birds. All this is of interest to me, but it is not why I return to the lower Endrick, the part navigable in my kayak, again and again.

I approach the mouth of the river from the lochside village of Balmaha, about half a mile to the north. Along this stretch of shoreline, in spring, the over-wintering Greenland-white-fronted geese are still to be seen, so too are the Canada geese which stay all year. My silent passage in a kayak hardly disturbs them, allowing a close look. Near the river's mouth the bay is thick with water-lilies. I push through softly resisting acres of bright green waxy leaves, spread flat on the surface, and fleshy stems supporting large-petalled pink, white or yellow flowers. Rushes screen the entrance to the river, making it hard to find. As my bows part them, they sway and whisper. The river is about four to six feet below the level of the meadows and woodland along its banks, sheltered from the wind. Even on blustery days, this slow-moving stretch of water can be flat calm. The resulting reflections are, for me, one of the Endrick's greatest attractions. At times, it is hard to tell where the river bank ends and its mirror image begins; which are fallen limbs of trees and which their reflections. The beauty of this riparian regime, the trees and the variety of plants and shrubs, is enjoyed twice over – both in the real world and in its upside-down reproduction, the latter often enhanced by a slight refraction and the merest shimmer from the flow. And then there are the skies. Archie, my usual companion on these jaunts, says that skimming through the billowing clouds is like when you dream you're flying.

The steep red banks are home to hundreds of sand martins (members of the swallow family), which emerge from their tunnels to swoop and dart above me. Cows and horses gaze down on me with big brown eyes; and the clumps of giant hogweed[3] appear even more immense than they really are. Many are as much as seven to ten feet tall, marvels of natural engineering, with their hollow, ribbed stems, topped by cartwheel spokes and umbrellas of white flowers. Being non-native and invasive, many people regard the giant hogweed as a noxious weed to be eradicated, but every trip I make up the Endrick I look forward to being awed by these spectacular plants all over again. In places, trees overhang the riverbank, creating archways and cool, green tunnels through which a slim kayak can thread its way.

This lower section of the river loops back on itself repeatedly, so that it is not uncommon to find myself passing very close to where I was twenty minutes earlier. One happy result of this meandering is that nothing stays in the same place for long. Conic Hill and Ben Lomond which were on my left moments ago, appear ahead of me, then over my right shoulder. I enjoy sliding through scatterings of floating leaves in all their autumnal glory and winter's frost-sharpened shapes. The Endrick is a river for all seasons.

Loch Coruisk: the one-eyed witch of the west.
On 'The Isle of Mists' I am not often granted a clear view of the Cuillin peaks. Frequently they are half shrouded, dark, austere and stern, and yet alluring, like a dusky maiden performing the Dance of the Seven Veils, revealing tantalising glimpses through vapour layers – hints of bare, bristling ridges, spires, crags, gullies, deeply gouged corries and long scree slopes. The Black Cuillin give the impression of being one enormous, solid, sculptured stone. Their coarse, crystalline gabbro provides so much friction that I can saunter, hands in pockets, up steep-angled rock. Even with sheets of water sliding down them, I have crossed sloping slabs, so pitted and abrasive that all fears of a slip are banished. Sunk deep in these hills is Loch Coruisk, a remote, wild place. Around it, in a horseshoe, swing the twenty peaks of the Black Cuillin. Intensified by the enclosing, near-perpendicular cliffs is the scent of bog myrtle and rain-sweet heather. At night, echoing mournfully across this dark bowl, is a fox's lonely cry. The Cuillin has been called 'the most beautiful witch of the western seas.' Beautiful undoubtedly, and witchlike too, with sharp talons piercing the sky, and unpredictable weather brewed in high rock cauldrons. Loch Coruisk is the witch's single eye, its all-seeing eye. On most days the loch lies still, unblinking, unruffled by winds that buffet the summits, reflecting the encircling mountains and their many moods, the changing sky, the moon, or the Northern Lights. Sometimes it brims with burnished silver, spilling liquid starlight; at other times it's black with unfathomable mystery. I return to the Cuillin and Loch Coruisk whenever I can, for the one-eyed witch has cast her spell on me, a spell that brings an undying hunger of the heart.

The Great Forest Of Ard
The Great Forest of Ard is part of the Queen Elizabeth Forest

Park, established in 1953, the year of the coronation of Elizabeth II. And this park is itself part of the Loch Lomond and Trossachs National Park. The Great Forest of Ard extends west from the attractive village of Aberfoyle towards the rugged hills beside Loch Lomond, and includes Loch Ard, which is about two and a half miles long, and the slightly smaller Loch Chon (pronounced 'Shaun').

It is something of a hidden treasure, boasting no less than seventeen different species of conifer alongside remnants of ancient oaks. Wildlife includes red and roe deer, pine martens, otters, red squirrels, the reintroduced water voles, barn owls and capercaille. It has a sculpture trail. Giant water insects seem to hover over the water; huge fish to leap from the loch and a family of foxes, in silver metal, haunt the woods.

My friend, Archie, and I drive there often from Helensburgh. In summer we go for the kayaking and in autumn for the walks and the magnificent autumn colours.

The road, which will eventually take you to Loch Katrine (if you branch right) and to Inversnaid on the eastern shores of Loch Lomond (if you turn left), passes along the northern shores of Loch Ard. Launch places are hard to find and involve carrying the kayaks over a low wall. However, once on the water, the rewards are plentiful. Surrounded by forest with views of Ben Lomond, Ben Venue and Beinn Bhreac (there are three other mountains by the same name in the area), chains of little islands to wander in and out of and, on the southern uninhabited side, little coves and beaches to land for picnics, or to stretch cramped legs along the footpaths, a summer day can pass very pleasantly indeed.

One of our favourite sections is Milton Basin at the very eastern end of the loch, reached by a narrow channel from the main body of Loch Ard. The channel is too shallow for any craft except a kayak. It's overhung by branches from either bank, forming, in summer, a leafy archway beneath which winds a greenly dappled water lane. I remember, one rainy day, my bows gently pushing through rushes, making a rustling sound that matched the whispering rain. Then emerging into Milton Basin with its meadows of water lillies, blooming in whites and yellows, their large waxy leaves, flat on the calm surface, gathering raindrops into abstract shapes, while all around concentric circles spread out, overlapped, renewed.

Going in the other direction we once encountered a group of wild swimmers – a fairly recent addition to the perch, pike and brown trout that already inhabit the loch. They were setting out for a small island about a mile away, which was the site of Duke Murdoch's Castle. Once a fortified tower, possibly from the fourteenth century, it is now in ruins. The swimmers towed floats with them so that they could stop for a rest.

The Forest of Ard's autumn colours are breathtaking! The variety of deciduous trees and shrubs all in a slightly different phase of their seasonal cycle creates a wonderful display. To oak, mountain ash, hazel and birch in their last glorious displays before their leaves fall, are added brambles; bushes that flare so brightly that they could almost be the Biblical burning bush; ferns that progress through green, yellow and ever-deepening browns; and large clumps of moss which turn a range of rich reds in autumn. The seventeen different species of conifer include varieties of both pine and fir, each with its own shade of green: emerald, olive, seaweed, greens that are almost blue and some that are almost black. Then there are the evergreen rhdodendrons, a native of Nepal, which have escaped from the gardens of country houses and are now a feature of many of our forests, The waxy, shiny brightness of their leaves contrasts with the firs' softer textures and contributes further to the panoply of greens. Add to this mix the European larch, one of the few conifers to shed its needles in preparation for winter. In doing so, it flames yellow and gold.

On still days it's hard to tell where the land ends and the loch begins. Land and loch are one rich, blazingly brilliant palette of nature's colours. Do you wonder that I come here often?

North Ronaldsay

Compared to the Hebrides or Shetland, the Orkneys are lush and fertile. As the old saying goes: 'An Orcadian is a farmer with a boat, while a Shetlander is a fisherman with a croft.' As our car topped one of the rolling hills on Mainland Orkney we could see islands spread out like shards of broken pottery, island upon island. The sense that there is always something more, something beyond the next island, or round the next headland, is one of the lures of Orkney. Fourteen of the islands are inhabited, but exactly how many islands there are depends on one's definition of an island. To an Orcadian, it is a piece of land on which you can keep a sheep for a year. Smaller than that and it's called a rock. The most northerly of the Orkneys is North Ronaldsay.

I have only been to North Ronaldsay once, but it is a place I visit in my dreams, a place I return to in my imagination, a place I want to share with other people. One day in early August I took the 15-minute flight there in an eight-seater plane from Kirkwall. Flying over the low-lying islands of Shapinsay, Stornsay, Eday and Sanday, I passed over crofts and a patchwork of fields. Between islands I looked down on translucent shallows. Golden sandbars with pearly white frills from the breaking waves, and green and amber seaweeds, not far from the surface, made the sea turquoise, emerald, lapis lazuli – the work of a master jeweller.

Moving beyond the tiny one-hut airport, I set out to walk round the island, but one hour later had progressed no more that 200 yards. There was so much to look at and photograph – old zig-zag dry stones walls etched with lichens, fields of oats and barley rippling in the wind, flowered meadows like mediaeval tapestries, seals basking on the off-shore rocks; always the vast skies like a great dome over this flat landscape; and the salt sea scent.

A 13-mile stone wall runs round the island. Its purpose is not to keep the sheep in, but to confine them to the narrow stretch of beach between the wall and the sea where they live on seaweed. Domesticated ruminants like cows and sheep, graze by day, then regurgitate the semi-digested cud and chew this by night to complete the digestive processes. TheNorth Ronaldsay sheep, however, have evolved in a different way. Their digestive cycle is determined by the tides so that they graze on the seaweed when it is exposed at low-tide, the regurgitate and chew the cud when their food is covered at high-tide.

I stopped for my packed lunch near an abandoned fisherman's cottage, draped with drying nets. Beside it was the skeleton of a four-oared boat, known by Orcadians as a *fowererns,* from which line fishing was done.

Further round the coast is the lighthouse. On a clear day, the Fair Isles can be seen from the top; and then a stop at the Bird Observatory, set up in 1987 to study and record the migrant birds that each year pass through Okney's most northerly island. The number and variety of birds arriving here on migration can be spectacular. The records for most years show figures of close on 150 different species passing through.

I suppose I was just passing through, too. Like the birds, I have a strong instinct to return.

NOTES

1 Not to be confused with Gairloch in Wester Ross.

2 Lampreys, which look rather like eels, are an ancient type of fish without jaws, scales or bones and quite unlike any other fish found in Britain.

3 Be warned that the sap of the giant hogweed (sometimes called giant cow parsley) causes severe skin burns, and possibly blindness if it comes in contact with the eyes.

MEDITATIONS IN THE WILDERNESS

For a quarter of a century I have been practising meditation. Every day, for about twenty minutes, I sit, with my eyes shut, in a relaxed position (not the lotus position which I find uncomfortable) and try to empty my mind until I pass into a stage of complete blankness and nothingness. Emerging on the other side of this, I am relaxed, stress-free and refreshed, my mind is clearer and more focused; my pulse and blood pressure are lower than normal, taking about one hour to return to their usual levels. I have definitely not been asleep, but in some other state of consciousness. I couldn't say where it is that I have been. I only know that I have a strong sense of having returned from a place where there is harmony and beauty. Sometimes this vanishing into nothingness comes quicker than others; sometimes it doesn't happen at all, as unbidden thoughts chase around my mind. But this, too, I find beneficial because it feels as if my subconscious mind has released things that needed to surface. What I have described is very much on the lower rungs of the transcendental meditation ladder. On the top rungs are those who have dedicated their lives to meditation, such as Buddhist lamas, Hindu holy men and hermits and early Christian monks, and at the other end are the likes of me.

W H Murray was a mystic, who practised transcendental meditation. In my biography of him I explain a bit more about this:

They [the major religions and philosophies of the world] teach that this ultimate harmony (or Reality, Pure Awareness, or Absolute Truth and Beauty, or God) is beyond the intellect alone – the word is not the thing it describes, the menu is not the food… [But] Reality can be realised through transcendental meditation... [which] transcends or goes beyond the physical, observable world to a spiritual state where glimpses of the Truth are possible. Scholars of mysticism strongly emphasise that, although it gives a direct connection to the Divine Essence, it is definitely not a short-cut. Great effort, hardship and discipline are required. Only then, says the author of *The Cloud of Unknowing,*[1] 'Will He sometimes peradventure send out a beam of ghostly light, piercing the cloud of unknowing that is betwixt thee and Him.'

In my own experience from the lower rungs, most of my deeper meditations have been associated with being close to nature. The author Stephen Graham, describes his own response to nature: 'As you sit on the hillside, or lie prone under the trees of a forest, or spread wet-legged by a mountain stream, the great door that does not look like a door, opens.'[2]

'Piercing the cloud of unknowing' seems to occur more easily after activities in which I have been completely absorbed by the physical and mental challenge and the exercise of skill – that is to say, when I have been in the flow.[3] I have experienced this kind of flow both as a climber and as a kayaker. Csikszentmihalyi, in his work *Flow: The Psychology of Optimal Expression,*[4] says there is a strong connection between being in the flow and meditation. People who experience flow report that it enhances their ability to achieve meditation; and people who have found a path to deep meditation also find that they experience flow more regularly than otherwise. Even without experiencing flow, I find that contact with the natural environment around me aids meditation. It works the other way round, too. Soon after I had taken up meditation, my ability as a kayaker dramatically improved. No longer did I see the ocean and the elements as something to be battled against with a clenched jaw and white knuckles. Instead, I felt a new sense of oneness with the ocean, I relaxed and, as a result, became a better paddler.

Each person meditates in a different way; and for each person every meditation is different, as I shall try to show from my description of three of my own meditations:

One day in late March I went for a walk in a part of the oak forest that covers the rolling hills of Umbria. I was following small paths and carrying my camera. Sometimes I was intensely in the present, in the now, noticing every detail, all five senses alert, photographing the beauty around me from every angle and on a range of scales from the wide panorama across the forest, to the detail on the bark of a tree. At other times I allowed my thoughts to drift wherever they cared to go. Some of my best ideas bubble up while I am walking in the hills or paddling my kayak. I think it is something to do with a steady rhythm, and thoughts being stimulated by the slowly changing scene. I alternated between two different kinds of creativity – being in the present, camera and mind in focus, and being mentally elsewhere, the mind producing new ideas and connections. It was like some mental equivalent to stepping out of a sauna into the pool and then back again several times – invigorating and relaxing both at once. So, when, on the way home, I came to the edge of the forest, I was, you might say, 'warmed up' for my session of meditation. In sunshine I descended through a terraced olive grove which overlooked the farmland spread out below. I came upon an area richly carpeted with what looked like oxeye daisies, except that they were purple and not white. I sat with my back to a low terrace wall. Below me and about half a mile away, a tractor was chug-chugging in a field; smoke drifted upwards from a bonfire, its faint tang mixing with the forest scents reaching me from the slopes above. From somewhere closer came the steady snip-snip of an olive tree being pruned. Small birds were in full voice, like sound-stars twinkling or bright bubbles in a lazy river. Near my left foot a tiny beetle ascended the trunk of an olive tree, negotiating the crevices in the bark and the patches of brown, white and yellow lichen.

I closed my eyes and softly repeated my 'mantra' – a two-syllable, vibrating sound that has no meaning. Breathe out on the first syllable, breathe in on the second syllable. I tried not to think of anything except my breathing, to still the internal chatter of my brain. Out went my breath to become part of this planet's atmosphere. Perhaps, centuries from now, particles of that breath will still be in circulation. Breathe in. I think: 'Maybe I'm drawing into my body a tiny particle of breath exhaled by a creature now extinct, or perhaps by the Buddha himself.' A sense of being part of something vastly older and bigger than myself began to steal over me. A picture of the beetle entered my mind. That olive tree is its whole world, its whole universe. It has no idea its tree is part of an orchard, or that the orchard is just a small area of one hillside in a range of hills. Gradually my mind pulled back, a zoom lens in reverse. My worries became more and more distant and insignificant until, in the grander scheme of things, they ceased to exist. The sounds of the birds, the tractor, the clippers melded into harmonious, sweet music. A sense of the unity of everything was strongly upon me. Now I was hardly aware of my breathing. In… out. My mind emptied, but it would be incorrect to say I was thinking of nothing, because even to be thinking of nothing and to be focusing on dispelling wayward thoughts and distractions is to be thinking of something. The mind has simply to relinquish control, to let go and allow itself to be emptied until the self vanishes.

The Garvellachs, or, to give them their Gaelic name, Hinba (pronounced Eenba), the Isles of the Sea, are four small islands in line astern between Jura and the south coast of Mull. The largest and southernmost of these, Eileach an Naoimh, was where Archie and I planned to camp for the night. The earliest stone buildings to survive in Scotland from the Christian era are on the eastern side of this island, built in the ninth century on the site of the little wooden monastery founded in the sixth century in the name of St Brendan. St Colomba of Iona used the Hinba monastery as a 'desert' or retreat. We landed and erected our tent near the ruins, close to the beehive constructions which were used as cells by the monks and solitaries of the Celtic Church. There is something very special about the Garvellachs. They emanate the same aura of spirituality that many people have felt on Iona. I settled down to meditate, resting against one of the stone beehive cells. The evening had that rare quality of light unique to the Western Isles. On the exposed western side of the island Atlantic rollers were crashing against the cliff, distant, muffled, a slow, regular pulse. My own pulse and my breathing slowed until it kept time with the ocean. My mind drifted to earlier in the day. Approaching the Garvellachs in our kayaks the ocean was like a magical undulating landscape, or the deep, slow breathing of some vast slumbering beast. Up on a swell, down into a trough… and down… and down into a deep, peaceful, refreshing place. When I opened my eyes, I pondered whether the ease with which I had slipped away into nothingness had something to do with those monks. Had the calm and tranquillity they had engendered reached out to me across the centuries, or could it be that those early saints chose these islands because they sensed other forces already there?

The kayaking that day in the Nuuk Fjords of Greenland, surrounded by snow-capped mountains, had been superb. It was one of those days when the sea conditions were hard enough to be really testing, but not quite crossing that line where the tingle of excitement and the joy of mastery and achievement turns to fear. Soon after landing, the skies unleashed volleys of rain and hail, and we struggled to erect our tents with frozen fingers. Once inside my tent, I sat propped up against a pile of waterproof bags, appreciating the warmth and shelter and the contrast with conditions outside. A blast of hail drummed on the fabric overhead. Several weeks before coming to Greenland I had been given an audiotape, the sounds of nature set to classical music 'for relaxation and meditation' – ocean surf, rain, thunderstorm, flowing water, the call of whales. They were all here: the mountain stream in the gorge to my right, waves breaking against the cliffs a hundred feet below me, the patter of the hail, and, perhaps not a thunderstorm, but the grumbling, rumbling icebergs instead. These sounds gradually merged with my heartbeat into one all-embracing harmony. And the whales were out there somewhere. Maybe, at a subliminal level, their signals were reaching me. In Buddhist paintings lamas and holy men are sometimes depicted carrying a bell that represents the perfect sound of voiceless wisdom. These sounds, which now whispered to my senses, contained that kind of wisdom.

NOTES

1 *The Cloud of Unknowing* is a book by an anonymous fourteenth-century English author, a book which Aldous Huxley describes as 'one of the finest flowers of medieval mystical literature.' The author of *The Cloud of Unknowing* counsels his readers not to seek God through knowledge but by spiritual union with Him through the heart.

2 Stephen Graham, *The Gentle Art of Tramping* (Ernest Benn, 1927).

3 Flow theory and the work of Csikszentmihalyi is also discussed in the essay 'Because It's Daft'
.
4 Milhaly Csikszentmihalyi, F*low: The Psychology of Optimal Expression* (University of Chicago Press, 1983).

YOU

Sea-smoothed, salt-kissed, warm, wave-rounded rock:
Your skin, gold-dusted in the dawn.

Fathoms of twilight and translucence:
Your face in layered sleep.

Wind-rippled wild corn amongst the dunes:
Your tresses falling free.

 Lagoons of splintered light:
Your eyes now open to the day.

Ocean aglow with rising sun:
Your radiant, waking smile.

IN PRAISE OF THE COLOURS OF THE CLYDE

As a child, whenever I did a painting of the sea, it was invariably navy blue, just as tree trunks were brown, grass was green and the sky, well, obviously it had to be sky blue. Perhaps, in a headstrong moment, I might add a few wavy white lines to the sea, but that was pushing on the limits of what was known and safe. As an adult, almost daily for the last forty years, I have looked out of my study window across the Clyde Estuary and I have never ceased to marvel at the infinite variety of the colours of the sea. Here, in this tidal zone, where the river begins to broaden out to the sea, flanked by hills and in the path of Atlantic weather systems that bring a goodly amount of cloud and rain, greys tend to dominate. I didn't realise until I moved into this house on the water's edge how many kinds of grey there could be. We are all familiar with the title of that book (if not with its contents) *Fifty Shades of Grey.* From my study I see more shades than that – greys that range from silver to near black; greys which share boundaries with blues, hint at yellows, slide imperceptibly into purples and pinks, fade towards pale phantoms of grey, or by degrees graduate into greens.

I call upon slate to aid me in describing the seascape beyond my window: the grey-blue-greens of Welsh slate; flecked and veined Italian slate; Brazilian black; green-tinged Lakeland slate; from the quarries of Ballachulish, the hues of coal and charcoal and from those of the island of Belnahua slates which plumb the depths of blueness.

Now I must summon metallurgy to help me pin down those elusive greys, invoking precious metals such as silver and platinum; base metals like lead, tin and iron; the rare metalloid, antimony, with its lustrous sheen; and a host of alloys – pewter, gun-metal, chromium, aluminium, steel, spiegeleisen or mirror-iron; and many amalgams of mercury.

Then again, this stretch of estuary brings to mind the ink-wash paintings of the Chinese masters who used only varying densities of black, achieving in one brush stroke tones that ranged from deep black to silver grey. It is reminiscent, too, of certain canvases of Vermeer, Titian or Caravaggio, when employing their monochrome grisaille technique.

Mallards land in our garden every morning, seeking food and, at the end of winter, looking for places to nest. Natural inhabitants of these shores, they encompass in their feathers all the colours of the estuary on which they swim. I speak of the drakes. The ducks, the females, are a speckled brown to blend with the undergrowth amongst which they nest and lay their eggs. In the drakes' tail feathers are the blacks of the sea beneath thunder clouds, and the whites of foaming crests. Their reddish-brown chests are the colour one sees at low tide when waves crash on the beach, churning up the mud not far below. The area around the underside and middle of their bodies has that same pallor as appears on the water an hour before a misty dawn, a whispered message, a slight lifting of the darkness, rather than light itself. Then there's that small triangle on the upper back, between the wings, which is mottled and dappled like wind-ruffled patches where a breeze finds passage through a gap in the hills. Above this dappled down is the drake's iridescent neck: the emerald green of sun-stroked seaweed floating on the surface; the midnight blue of waves shimmering in the starlight; and the orange-yellow beak – the path laid across the water by a melon moon.

Today, in January, with the morning sun still low in the sky, and a layer of bruised cloud hiding the hill-tops, the scene is like an antique black and white photograph that has been tinted sepia, fading and blotching as the silver sulphide salts unevenly deteriorate. There are darker areas where the overhead clouds are thicker and browner. Where the sun's rays break through are streaks of brass; bands of gold, aureate, clinquant and coruscating; and creamy frills where the washes of passing ships reach the shore. If the Chinese masters had used sepia ink-washes, this morning's scene might have flowed from their brushes. The greyish tones, though, are never far away, lurking in the corners of my eye.

I think the closest I can come to describing this generosity of greys is to write about my family's blue-grey eyes. Blue-grey, but flecked with many tints and pinpoints of scattered light; polychromic eyes which alter in hue and tone, in depth and intensity, in brightness and sparkle according to mood, health, or fleeting thoughts; eyes which can be clear or clouded, cold or softly warm; eyes which reflect the world and are windows onto the soul.

I have heard people use the phrase, 'a melancholy of greys.' Like grey itself, the word 'melancholy' has shades of meaning, including sombre, gloomy, sullen – all of which have, on occasions, applied to the square mile of sea I gaze upon from my house. It's not the sea, of course, which has these moods - it creates them in the human mind. Such melancholy is not typical of the emotions the grey tones of the Clyde evoke in me. If I could choose a collective noun for greys, rather than 'melancholy,' it would be 'an astonishment of greys', for their subtle, ceaseless shade-shiftings are a source of endless fascination, surprise, wonder and joy. I have thrilled to the wine-coloured Mediterranean at sunset. I have marvelled at bays lapping with liquid jade in Hawaii and the South China Sea. In the Outer Hebrides I have known the magic of white sand shallows holding turquoise lagoons. Arctic waters of pure, pellucid sapphire are precious memories, as is the ocean afire under a midnight sun. But I am content, more than content, with the greys of the Clyde Estuary. I have not tired of them, nor shall I.

IN PRAISE OF SMALL ISLANDS

I mean really small islands I can walk round in under an hour and can view in their entirety from one spot; islands small enough to give life simple, manageable proportions and on which time vanishes, so absorbing is their exploration; islands which arouse a sense of ownership – not so much that I have claimed them, although that is true, but that they have claimed me. For their siren call to fully work upon me, for them to awaken my inner Crusoe, they have to be uninhabited – desert islands in the true meaning of the phrase. In this praise song in prose to small islands many beautiful places must go unmentioned. If I write only of six or seven islands, they are here to represent and stand in for dozens more, such as Mousa in Shetland with its magic caves and Iron Age broch; far out Copinsay in Orkney, remote and wild; the wonderful archipelagos of the Summer Isles and the Monach Isles; the bare, sculptured rocks and seal colonies of North Rona; Belnahua with its ghost village.

The smallest island I have ever camped on is in Loch Lomond. It is flat, almost perfectly round and, depending on the level of the water in the loch at the time, about four feet in radius, covered in coarse grass and hardly more than a foot above the surface of the loch. Orcadians define an island as a piece of land on which you can feed a sheep for a year. Smaller than that, they say, it's a rock. This island wouldn't feed a sheep for a day, let alone a year. It did support a couple of beetles, though. A little brown bird, slightly smaller than a house sparrow, which might have been a female pied flycatcher, fluttered in to gather crumbs from my meal. The weather was perfect for sleeping in the open and the breeze just sufficient for the midges not to be a problem. That night, with a half moon laying a beam across the loch, I watched three deer swim from a nearby island to the mainland. Maps attach no name to this scrap of land that barely breaks the surface of the loch. Sometimes, after heavy rain, when the water level rises, it isn't there.

An island which vanishes more frequently than the one in Loch Lomond is the low and bluish cockle bank in the Clyde Estuary. Strictly speaking, it is not an island since it is above the water for only about six hours in the twelve-hour tidal cycle. This is the fascination of it: its ephemeral nature and the way it relentlessly diminishes until the point of disappearance. Small hollows and valleys fill up, dividing the cockle bank into clusters of islands; the gaps between them become deeper, wider, the islands smaller and smaller. The flow and flux of the flood's penetrating fingers keep the mini-coastlines in a state of constant change. If I close my eyes for a few minutes the scene is utterly transformed when I open them again. Finally, one small top remains with me and my kayak on it. The kayak begins to float. I stand knee deep in water, feeling the mud and cockle-shells beneath my feet. It is time to go. But I know I will be back before long for another performance.

The Treshnish Isles are a chain of small islands lying to the west of Mull. One of these is Lunga. Our approach to it in kayaks was marked by the splash of seals taking to the water, and erupting colonies of seabirds. They rose in clouds, circling suspiciously above us, shrieking and swooping. These islands are the winter quarters of up to a thousand barnacle geese, but this was summer and it was the puffins, guillemots, razorbills, kittiwakes, fulmars, terns, cormorants and gulls which gave us noisy greeting. The twenty-five species of seabirds which breed regularly on the Treshnish Isles play a big part in maintaining the herb-rich pastures. The last permanent inhabitants left in 1824, but sheep graze on this treeless island, keeping the grass short and springy. The rain clouds of the afternoon had disappeared. It was a fine evening. Without unpacking our kayaks we hurried to Lunga's 337-foot summit to catch the last hours of daylight. Lunga is one and a quarter miles long and 600 yards wide at its broadest point. From the summit we could see the Paps of Jura forty miles to the south-east and the Cuillins of Skye sixty miles to the north. Looking westward, with the sun sinking into the Atlantic behind Tiree, I could understand why the Norsemen bestowed the name Haubredey – the Isles on the Edge of the Sea. Skirting the edge of a tall cliff we looked down on steep-sided Dun Cruit, the harp-shaped rock in the sea. Its wild music was the noise of seabirds in their thousands, the wind and the pounding Atlantic rollers. After a supper cooked over a driftwood fire, I pitched my tent near the ruined houses whose rounded corners and dry-stone walls were not of this or the previous century. From their underground burrows rose the babbled of storm petrels. I thought about the sunset view from the summit and began counting in my mind all the islands I had seen from there: Jura, Colonsay, Iona, Staffa, Ulva, Gometra, Bac Beag, Bac More… I had reached nineteen when I fell asleep.

Loch Maree in Wester Ross is, for kayakers, one of the most richly rewarding of Scotland's inland lochs. Amongst its dozens of fascinating islands is the little gem, the Isle of Maree, sometimes known as the Sacred Isle of the Moon because of its Druid circle, dated at 100 BC. The island is believed to be the eighth-century hermitage of Saint Maol Rubha. It has the remains of a chapel and there are ancient stands of oak and holly trees no longer found on the other islands in the loch. As late as the eighteenth century, being towed round the island behind a boat was believed to be a cure for mental illness. Local tradition says that nothing must ever be taken from the island, not even a pebble from the shore, in case the insanity, which was 'cured' here, be returned to the outside world. An offering was made on behalf of the patient by nailing a rag or a ribbon to the Wish Tree, or by driving a coin into it edgewise. Most of the coins wedged into the knotted fibres of the tree are now blue-green with mould, the oldest ones still there going back to early Victorian times. The original Wish Tree is still standing, a gnarled, sinewy old oak that died many years ago of copper poisoning. The feeling that pagan spirits still lurk in these woods is palpable, a feeling enhanced by the proximity of the larger Eilean Subhain where there is a small hidden loch, and on that loch there is yet another island - an island within an island, a legendary place where on certain nights of the year the queen of the fairies is said to hold court. Landlubbers say that all kayakers are mad. After paddling round the Isle of Maree was I cured? What do you think? I didn't remove anything from the island, but I did leave behind a wish that one day I might return.

On the morning of 28 January 1974, a new landmark appeared in the Clyde Estuary. A Greek cargo ship lay on her side between Helensburgh and Greenock. An island called *Captayanis*. During the night, in a gale, the *Captayanis* had dragged her moorings and drifted in heavy seas before colliding with a tanker and being holed. In a bid to save his ship, the Greek captain deliberately ran her onto a sandbank. As 8,000 tons of sugar dissolved into the Clyde, the captain bowed to the inevitable and ordered the ship to be abandoned. Slowly, the deserted ship settled onto her side, coming to rest at a perfect ninety degrees to her upright position. The *Captayanis* lies there to this day, in mid-estuary. Her underside is turned towards the Greenock shore, her decks face Helensburgh, the bows point upriver, while beyond the stern are the wild hills of Argyll. About four months after the Captayanis ran aground I paddled out to her with the intention of spending the night aboard. Clouds of seabirds rose at my approach. Her mast lay exactly along the waterline, ship and tide in perfect equilibrium. Slowly I cruised round the wreck. Decks were walls, walls were decks, while ladders walked horizontally into space. A hatch opened like a window into the cavernous hull. I peered inside – black, black water, the stench of oil and rust and a hollow, dripping sound. The starboard bow reared high, but gently sloped at the waterline like a little beach. I paddled round to what had been the ship's flat bottom, now iron cliffs of rusty brown, then completed the circuit, passing the giant seaweed-covered rudder and barnacled propeller. Extracting myself from my kayak and climbing onto the wreck proved difficult. Finally, I was standing on what had once been the side of the hull, amazed at how flat it was. I wandered over the steel-riveted plateau, admiring the 360 degree panorama from the middle of the estuary. Ringed by twinkling lights, I ate my meal. Then, moving to the bridge, I climbed through an opening and dropped into the wheelhouse. In the centre of the floor was a porthole; in the middle of one wall a door opened like a letter-box. The wheel itself, the compass and other instruments of navigation were gone. After the storm had abated, swarms of little boats clustered round the dead ship. In a matter of days, furniture, fittings, anything movable had disappeared. I unrolled my sleeping-bag and prepared for sleep. It was dark, it was cold. The ship let out a long, deep sigh. I listened intently. She rumbled and echoed and sobbed. The changing tide, I told myself. Volumes of air and water shifting inside her, I told myself, but I was not convinced. Dawn was breaking. The sea was flat calm; and the gulls were resting in their hundreds on the hull. Since that first visit I have returned to the *Captayanis* many times. Every year the reds and browns of rust are more apparent, she is a little greener about the waterline and whiter from the attentions of the birds. In her primitive soil of bird-droppings windblown dust and peeling paint moss and grass have taken root, sea pinks and daisies bloom. I have grown fond of the iron island in the Clyde.

Out Stack lies just over a mile north of the island of Unst in Shetland and a few hundred yards north of Muckle Flugga (called North Unst until 1964). On a big but friendly swell we paddled first to Muckle Flugga (which translates as big steep-sided island), under a sky thick with gannets. Most boats make use of the small stone jetty, but only in calm weather. Unfortunately, the top of the jetty was too high to be of any help to a kayaker trying to land, and the sea was far from calm.

The trick was to get the timing right. One by one we waited for the right moment, then made a quick dash to a slot between two rocks at the base of the cliff, followed by a wild scramble to get out before the next big wave crashed in. We climbed 200 feet to the base of the lighthouse up flights of aluminium stairs fixed to the cliff. The lighthouse is yet another built by Thomas Stevenson (father of Robert Louis Stevenson). It was completed in 1858 and manned until 1995 when it was automated. Although its base is 200 feet above the sea, in winter gales the sea not only brakes heavily over the tower, but once burst open the door of the dwelling room, as well as carrying off a large section of the stone wall around the lighthouse. From our vantage point at the base of the tower we had a magnificent view across the tide-ripped stretch of water to the Hermeness peninsula of Unst. On its tall cliffs is one of the UK's largest puffin colonies. It was on these cliffs that the great skua made a comeback from near extinction. We agreed that where we now stood would be a great place to witness the marreel – a word from the old language of the Shetlands, meaning the bright glow of phosphorescence on the sea, best seen in winter when the light is low and when a storm force wind meets a strong current head on. It was easy to imagine that this might have been the Ultima Thule of the ancient Greeks, the northern most habitable region of the world. To the medieval geographers the name simply meant a distant, mysterious place beyond the boundaries of the known world. As we headed for Out Stack, it seemed like an apt description. Out Stack is a small roundish, rocky outcrop, the most northerly island in the British Isles. Its sides were too steep and the swell too large for us to land. Instead, each of us threw a pebble onto it, so that something of us, at least, had touched it. As we rounded Out Stack there was a thrill in knowing that, at that moment, we were the most northerly people in the British Isles. If I paddled East my first landfall would be Norway; going West across the North Atlantic it would be Greenland, while to the North nothing but ocean lay between me and the North Pole.

It has been my experience that the extent to which an island reveals its character and soul is in inverse proportion to its size. The smaller it is, the more intense has been my contact with it, the greater the intimacy. I am more acutely aware of its features. I explore every nook, inlet and cranny; I study the plants more closely, investigate the tidal pools and examine the rock strata. On islands such as these 'everything beckons us to perceive it'[1] Part of the attraction of islands of this size is the extraordinary quality of light. With no hills to block light from above, and being set in the midst of a reflecting sea, the air is luminous. For me, though, their greatest lure is that they fit inside my heart.

NOTES

1 I am indebted to Julian Hoffman for drawing my attention to this quote in his book *The Small Heart of Things*. The line comes from a poem with that title by Rainer Maria Rilke and was written between 1913-1920.

IN PRAISE OF RAIN

When I am making plans for a day on the hills or on the water, a forecast of rain is seldom a reason for gloom, or for cancelled plans. On both sea and land it has its own attractions and creates its own special moments. Three outings will serve to illustrate what I mean.

One Sunday in July, in Shetland, we paddled up Whale Firth and round the north end of Yell to Cullivoe. My outstanding memory of that day is of a spectacularly heavy cloudburst which lasted for nearly an hour. The surface of the water, as far as the eye could see, was pearl-encrusted with raindrops which flattened the waves and turned the seascape into something akin to a loudly hissing, undulating, frosted prairie. At times, sky and sea seemed almost to merge into one watery element; and I, in the midst of it, was exhilarated. So loud was the drumming on my deck that my whoops of excitement were barely audible. For about two hours after the heavens opened, massive volumes of water poured over the cliffs. Gushing torrents filled every gulley and groove, sluiced across slabs, became thundering waterfalls at every overhang. As if in imitation of this superabundance of flowing water, veins of quartz, ten feet wide or more in places, criss-crossed the cliffs. We found a sea-cave to shelter in, having first passed through the mini-Niagra which screened its entrance. The rain stopped, the sun shone and a rainbow arched across the horizon. Later, when we landed in a remote bay, the rain began again. I lay on my back in a patch of thick, lush, wet vegetation and thought of Gerard Manley Hopkins' lines:

> What would the world be, once bereft
> Of wet and of wildness? Let them be left,
> O let them be left, wildness and wet;
> Long live the weeds and the wilderness yet.[1]

Closing my eyes, I let fat raindrops plop onto my eyelids. I opened my mouth. Rain splashed my teeth and tongue, and salty rivulets ran down my face and over my lips, tasting of the sea.

The Dubh-Uisage is a tributary of the River Falloch, joining it on its western side, just before it enters Loch Lomond's northern end. It was raining hard on that day in November, as it had been all week. It was exactly the right sort of day to walk beside a mountain burn and see it in all its might and glory, bursting with energy. Our usual crossing place was fairly low down where we could hop casually from boulder to boulder over a shallow trickle. Now, swollen by the rainfall, the burn was three or four times its normal width and in full spate, the stepping stones buried beneath the roaring water. The contrast between this dangerous, thrashing river and the benign burn we remembered was startling. We walked beside it, up a steep track, through mixed woodland, the forest fragrances magnified by the damp air. We drew level with the amphitheatre below the waterfall, now a churning cauldron, throwing up curtains of spray, their whiteness accentuated by the dark precipice behind. Over its rim the full-flooded river thundered with awesome power. Lunch was taken above the fall, our attention not on our sandwiches and flasks, but on the Dubh-Uisage hurtling over the edge, on the swirling mist and the drama in the booming amphitheatre below. The rain ceased, the clouds parted. From our perch we surveyed a glittering landscape. Fallen leaves, tree trunks, rocky outcrops and ephemeral pools all glinted and shone in their wetness. Raindrops, strung along the wires of a deer fence, glinted like glass beads; the texture and patterns on bark and rock were clearer, sharper; a narrow gulley choked with loose stones was transformed into an Aladdin's cave of precious jewels, so magically did their hidden colours emerge and glow.

On another occasion, after a prolonged period of rain in spring, the water level in Loch Lomond rose sufficiently to partially submerge some of the lower-lying islands. There is a dream-like quality about gliding in a kayak through woodland in bloom, the tree trunks rising sheer from the water, my bows pushing aside bobbing fir cones, my paddle strokes creating swirls of fallen petals; and paths, roots, bright green mosses and clumps of daffodils sliding by, beneath me.

I love walking on a path and seeing the sky reflected in freshly formed puddles. I love it when rain fills the landscape with the music of running water, gurgling, laughing, joyously singing. And I love the sound rain makes pattering on the fabric of my tent at night, when I am snug inside my sleeping-bag; the thrum and clatter of it on the tin roof of a mountain hut; or the way it smacks on leaves as it seeps through a forest canopy, and drips into still ponds, making ever-widening circles. I am with Thomas Merton in spirit when he wrote: 'What it is to sit absolutely alone, in the forest, at night, cherished by the wonderful unintelligible perfectly innocent speech, the most comforting speech in the world, the talk that rain makes by itself.'[2]

Provided I am properly dressed and shod for it, squelching through a sodden field has delights all of its own, as does splashing and sloshing through flooded ground, or shuffling through a drenched, thick mulch of leaves. Recently I discovered a new pleasure to be had from rain. When we arrived at the starting point for our walk, the skies had opened and rain was absolutely bucketing down. My companion and I didn't even open the car doors, but headed for a delightful tea-room and sat in comfy arm chairs, with steaming mugs of coffee and freshly baked scones, beside a glowing iron stove.

NOTES

1 From the poem 'Inversnaid,' 1918.

2 Thomas Merton (1915–1968) was an American mystic and Trappist monk. The quote is from his collection of essays, *Raids on the Unspeakable* (New Directions, 1966).

THE KINETIC LANDSCAPE

Later in this collection I argue strongly that there is no better way to fully appreciate a landscape than to be in it, part of it, experiencing it at the natural human pace and being able to stop and admire the details whenever one wants. However, for a majority of people in modern Britain, particularly urban dwellers – which is most of us – this is not how we experience landscape. For the most part we see it from a moving car, coach, train or aeroplane, the first of these being the most common. A friend, recently returned from his first visit to America, said to me, 'Everything I know about America comes from a moving screen.' He meant the windscreen of his hired car, the window of the train, and television and cinema screens. For me (and for everyone, I suppose), driving through a landscape is a very different experience from walking through it.[1] Despite the fact that there is a minimum of contact with anything outside my insulating capsule, I find that landscapes in motion have their own special delights.[2]

There is the obvious point that, on a drive in the country, I might average thirty or forty miles an hour, whereas, on foot, three or four miles an hour is likely to be my norm. Number of miles covered, in itself, is not necessarily a positive factor, but it is when it enables an increased panoramic perception. It allows me to see the contrasts between one area and another in a more immediate and sharper way than if I was walking the same route. The change from one kind of scenery to another arrives sooner and with greater impact. By being able to contrast barren moorland and lush valley, or steep-sided mountains and flat lowland my appreciation of each is enhanced. That seven-mile stretch of land covered on my walk can now be appreciated as part of a wider design and structure, part of what contributes to forming the character of the region as a whole. It is not often in a day's walk that I can follow the course of a river from its source to its end, seeing all its phases from turbulent youth, through middle-age, to its final sedate, meandering miles. In a car a lot is missed – the sound of the water, the flora and fauna along its banks, for instance – but other things are gained.

The plunge into or exit from a patch of mist or fog is more sudden and therefore more dramatic. The same is true of coming over the brow of a hill and seeing the ocean, or a green and fertile plain laid out below. In walking it is the slow anticipation; with driving it is the surprise. The experience of near and far is also quite different given greater speed, the time-span between tiny and imposingly large being short enough to create a sense of wonder. Especially at night, or with my eyes shut, when in rapid motion across the countryside, I feel its rhythms, its curves and contours, its rise and fall, the ripple and swell of its topography. Not all roads follow the natural line, and here are new rhythms, counter-rhythms and two-part harmonies.

What fascinates and attracts me most about viewing the countryside from the passenger-seat of a car is the way the vehicle somehow transfers its speed and energy to the landscape itself. Sometimes the ribbon of land on either side of the road becomes a river in full torrent, greens and browns and assorted shapes pouring and tumbling past the seemingly stationary viewer. If kinetic art is defined as art which depends on motion for its effect, then to combine spectator, fast-moving vehicle and landscape is to create a large-scale artistic 'happening.' Motion is the medium and beauty, as well as being in the eye of the beholder, is in his velocity. This applies to cityscapes as well. Reyner Banham, the British architecture and design critic, commented:

The language of design, architecture and urbanisation in Los Angeles is the language of movement. Mobility outweighs monumentality… and the city will never be fully understood by those who cannot move fluently through its diffuse urban texture, cannot go with the flow of its unprecedented life. So, like the earlier generation of English intellectuals who taught themselves Italian in order to read Dante in the original, I learned to drive in order to read Los Angeles in the original.[3]

Joy-riding through the kinetic countryside I am learning new ways of seeing.

I like how the foreground moves faster than the background; the way trees, buildings and other objects constantly change their spacial relationship to each other; and, if the road is curving, the way front, side and back are seen in quick-time – a fluid, shape-shifting scene of altering angles and juxtapositions. Side-roads and paths bend and unbend, writhing like snakes, while furrows and rows of crops spring open and snap shut in dizzying succession. I enjoy a low-lying sun dodging and winking behind a wood; and a full moon playing peek-a-boo, first on my right, now on the left, before hiding behind a hill, only to jump out again minutes later. There is enjoyment, too, in whizzing past stands of tall straight trees. My eye is gratified in the same sort of way as is my finger-nail when it zips across corrugated cardboard. In winter a row of leafless trees beside the road can blur into a flimsy veil, lending mystery and enchantment to what lies behind, half-hidden. If the roadside trees are spaced at regular intervals, the images flicker by as on a reel of film. I am in the best seat in the house, watching a movie. In fact, I'm watching the illusion of a movie, which, itself, is an illusion of movement. Ross Harley points out in his essay 'Motion Landscapes' that: 'the huge lines of spectators jostling for position at the movie-house may have all but disappeared, but they have merely reformed into the orderly lines of cars jostling the freeway each day at the same precise hour.'[4]

Modern technology has changed the way we see the environment. Artists are now attempting to reflect this in their work, adding a new dimension to landscape aesthetics. They try to express and interpret the kind of sensations I have been describing by using a variety of techniques such as mobile constructions powered by wind, water, gravity or solar cells; revolving platforms that convey the spectator past prepared images; time-lapse photography; innovative applications of digital imaging and virtual reality; moving wood and string installations which simulate the motion of a wave, the outward spreading rings from a raindrop plopping into water, or the eddies in a stream. I am happy to embrace all of this provided I can also dawdle by the riverbank, inhale deeply in a flower-rich meadow, feel rough ground, rather than a man-made surface, beneath my feet, or simply stand and stare.

NOTES

1.There is, of course, the matter of whether we should be travelling by carbon-emitting forms of transport and seeking more eco-friendly alternatives, but this is a subject for a different essay in a different kind of book.

2. For the duration of this essay my comments are as a passenger and not as a driver. I would hope that the latter is paying attention to the road and the traffic, rather than to the scenery.

3. Reyner Banham, *Los Angeles: The Architecture of Four Ecologies* (Penguin, 1973).

4. On the Australian website, 'Stereopresence.'

GREY WOLF HAUNTING

Echoing down the centuries
Hear the last wolf's lonely call.
Emptied land grey wolf haunting.
Out of balance and unwhole,
Empty land grey wolf wanting.
In these mountains, moors and glens,
At the margins, at the edge,
Demonized and killed,
Grey wolf, the hunter hunted,
Was so cruelly banished.

Amidst ash and birch which match
Flecked coat flits wolf's spirit.
In brindled mountain flanks where
Mists ghost towards grazing deer
Lies a story yet unfinished.
Wolf lives on in keening winds,
Rolling hills like loping run,
Deer-cropped plants but seldom seen -
Glimpse the shadow of a dream,
Aching absence of the vanished.

Grey wolf pads through our psyche,
The hunger, the gnawing need
For contact with otherness,
For wilderness and wildness
And nature replenished.
Echoing down the centuries
Hear the last wolf's lonely call.
Emptied land grey wolf haunting.
Out of balance and unwhole,
Empty land grey wolf wanting.

MAN IS NOT HIMSELF ONLY

For over half a century I have been trying to explain to myself why certain landscapes attract me more than others. This essay is an attempt, at a very personal and subjective level, to do just that. A full and final answer, I know before I start, is beyond reach. I have drawn my examples entirely from Scotland where I have lived for most of my adult life and whose landscapes I know more intimately than anywhere else. I discuss those types of landscape which appeal to me most – mountains, forests, rivers and especially coastlines. The last of these being, in my opinion, one of the greatest glories of Scottish landscape with over eight thousand miles[1] of sea cliffs, plunging waterfalls, caves, stacks, arches, white shell beaches, singing sands, dramatic tidal flows and an abundance of fascinating flora and fauna. Of urban landscapes, farmland and other areas where human intervention dominates I have here little to say, although I acknowledge that there, too, I have found beauty. My preference is for natural landscapes and for remote, wild places. Perhaps I should state, at this point that, except for the upper regions of the higher mountains and the Flow Country in Sutherland (the largest area of natural bog-land in Europe), all of Scotland's seemingly wild country is the result of human activity – a fact which led Dr Robert Lambert to comment: 'In Great Britain, and in Europe as a whole, wilderness is so far removed from our historical and cultural traditions that we have little understanding of what it should be in its purest form.'[2]

Trying to be objective about my subjectivity I would say that, for the most part, I see what I have been taught or conditioned to see. On car journeys my parents would exclaim in delight over certain types of scenery or disparage others, thereby fixing models in my mind of what was to be admired and what was not. Coach tours were much the same, stopping at pre-selected viewpoints where we were invited to gaze in wonder and click away with our cameras. I have observed that the surroundings of our childhood, our most impressionable and formative years, are the type of surroundings we tend to love most. Often, figuring large in this process are idealised memories of places where long summer holidays were spent. Imprinted on me are my schooldays in the forested Nilgiri Hills of southern India, a year living in the Himalayan foothills and sailing trips with my father to explore the Devon coast. So subjective is my perception of natural beauty that it can vary from day to day according to my mood or state of health. It has certainly changed with the transition from middle to old age. Whereas I once sought the wild beauty of the wilderness, I now look for gentler, quieter places. It is not so much a matter of declining physical ability as of a change in hormone balance. With the advancing years, as the balance of testosterone and oestrogen tips in favour of the latter, my natural instincts and inclinations have shifted in favour of more tranquil states of being.

My taste in scenery has also been shaped by the books I read in my youth: Richard Jeffries, James Fenimore Cooper, the Lakeland poets, Sir Walter Scott, Neil Gunn, Nan Shepherd, Albert Mummery, Leslie Stevens, Geoffrey Winthrop Young and later, W H Murray. These and other authors moulded my expectations of what an impressive landscape should look like. Even more influential were landscape paintings and photographs. They instructed me in what was to be looked at and looked for and they set the standard by which to judge the works of nature. After years of intimacy with the great outdoors it now seems to me that looking at the countryside as if it is a painting and judging it by the same artistic criteria is an approach fraught with problems. In the first place, paintings and photographs have frames and finite limits. Their confined view cannot show us the wider context and broader patterns. Pictorial representations of the countryside entirely miss out on what to me is one of its greatest delights – the fact that it is alive and changing from moment to moment, that it is in motion, it has a voice and place-specific fragrances.

By emphasising only the visual aspects of the landscape, by using only artistic criteria such as spatial composition, form and shape, proportion, colour and tone, light and shade we deny fuller and deeper definitions of the beautiful.

The invention of perspective as a tool for depicting three dimensional space has significantly shaped how we see the world around us and how we think of ourselves in relationship to it. It creates a single viewpoint for the spectator to perceive the image and in doing so it sets up a feeling that the spectator owns the view because all its components are structured and directed towards his eyes only. Viewed this way, landscape is observed and not participated in. We are on the outside, looking in. There is a distance and a barrier between the seer and the seen.[3] For me this is the main problem. To fully appreciate the beauty of a landscape or a seascape I need to be in it, part of it, engaged with it, moving through it, at one with it, experiencing it with all my senses.

Moreover, art-orientated models of the aesthetic appreciation of nature do not acknowledge the centrality of nature itself. Works of art are the creation of artists, but a landscape is the result of millions of years of change and development by natural processes and can only truly be appreciated on these terms. Hence the emergence of environmental or eco-aesthetics. This debate is part of the wider debate between the non-cognitive, mainly artistic and emotional, approach to nature and the cognitive approach. The latter suggests that an aesthetic appreciation of nature requires at least some knowledge of the natural sciences, especially geology, biology and ecology. It further suggests that, considering the level of human intervention in the British landscape, a grasp of how this has affected and altered it adds to our understanding of it, thereby enriching our appreciation. Whether or not the pleasure and the deeper understanding derived from this counts as an aesthetic experience is at the heart of the debate. My own subjective findings are that emotions and mind cannot be separated and that bringing together feeling and knowing, instinct and intellect is at the core of any serious aesthetic experience.

Some years ago I was walking in the upper reaches of Glen Loth, on the edge of the Flow Country. I was researching for a piece I was writing about the last wolf in Sutherland. Knowing the history of this added new meanings to the land. As well as what was present, there was an aching absence – an absence echoed by the ruined cottages of the Highland Clearances. Here was a deeper, sadder dimension to this valley's emptiness. In the Great Forest of Ard, the forest I visit most frequently, the autumn colours are superb. But there is so much more to it than this. Like any forest, it is a master-class in natural engineering and design, a statement in many forms that there is beauty in function, a marvel of patterns within patterns, of intersecting natural cycles on every scale; a self-healing, self-simulating system of amazing complexity that has achieved the seemingly impossible of reconciling unity and diversity, competition and co-operation, continuity and change. I have glimpsed but a fraction of the workings of this staggeringly wonderful super-organism. Even so, I know I have met a deeper kind of beauty. The ability to distinguish one type of tree from another eluded me for years. Had trees been huge animals I would surely not have remained so ignorant for so long. How much less interesting the world's fauna would have been to me if I had thought of them all as much the same. I used to scorn the need to name things. Putting a label on them, I said, did not make them any more beautiful. I feel now that I was wrong. Names and classifications allow insights into the family history and ecology of plants and animals, or into the forces and aeons it took to form the rocks around me. Names express the way the natural world is organised and tell me about the nature of nature itself.

What, for me, are the qualities and ingredients which make a landscape beautiful? Variety would be high on my list: places where one never knows what's around the next corner, a landscape full of irregularities and contrasts and which springs surprises on me; the kind of place where, as I move through it, valleys open up and close again, mountains show new faces and the relationships in space between one thing and another keep changing. I recall driving across California from Los Angeles to San Francisco. The crop on either side of the road was unvaried for hours at a time. Potatoes for two hours; then it changed abruptly and it was carrots for two hours. There was a certain fascination in watching the lines and furrows zip and unzip as I whizzed past; and the wide panorama would have made a good photograph, but, oh, the monotony!

I like wide open views such as one might obtain from a mountain top; and the long vista down a valley or a sea loch. Water of all kinds attracts me: the crash and churn of waves on a rugged coast; a tumbling burn; a flat calm loch making mirror images of the hills around. Scale, power and majesty induce in me a sense of awe: a mighty, thundering waterfall; the Corrievreckan tide-race, high cliffs, deep gorges and giant trees centuries old; and the bulk and mass of a mountain with its castles, ramparts and towers. On the other hand, the Appin hills are relatively low. They do not take the eye by storm but by grace of line and colour and haze and enchantment.

Although I find irregularity maintains interest, there is no denying that the human brain is a powerful pattern-recognising instrument and that we unconsciously look for patterns in everything. Cultivated fields, spread like a quilt, as seen from an aeroplane, are pleasurable to the eye. I am more excited, though, by nature's less obvious, hidden or half-hidden patterns. The essence of Earth's beauty lies for me, not in the symmetry of human design, but in disorder- a peculiarly organised and patterned disorder; in patterns which are too subtle, complex or on too large a scale to fully comprehend. Yet I sense they are there. This tension between order and chaos, this delicate balance, is fundamental to my concept of beauty. It is everywhere in nature, in the seemingly random arrangement of rocks and pebbles or dead leaves; in rushing water, in tangled vegetation and in the angles of fallen trees after a storm.

For me the sky is a major part of any landscape. Skyscapes may not be landscapes, but they are inseparable from them.

In their infinite variety clouds are one of the great miracles of this world. Possibly, in the whole history of our planet, no two clouds have ever been quite the same. What draws me to the low-lying Orkney Isles, more than any of their other attractions, is the vast dome of sky which gives such a strong sense of space and openness. Sky is one half of what determines the quality of light on land and sea. The other half being the nature of the surface the light is striking. 'Light is the doorway to emotion', wrote the renowned landscape photographer, Joe Cornish.[4] I especially love the low morning and evening light which bathes the land in gentle hues, throws long shadows and displays objects in strong relief. Sunset, sunrise, broad daylight, starlight, moonlight, snowlight, stormlight, raindrop lenses by the million; reflected light, soft, bright, filtered, dappled or hazy light, sparkle, shimmer, sheen and shine – the eloquence of light.

My list of ingredients is growing. I could go on, but I will confine myself to just three more. Encounters with wildlife definitely add to the impact an area makes upon me. They are part of the environment, fully adapted to it, at one with it, an expression of it. Leaping immediately to mind are the dolphins which surrounded my kayak and escorted me down the Sound of Mull; the large colonies of puffins and the seals on the Treshnish Isles; a large herd of deer undulating, flowing, over a red-brown hillside.

Pleasure in landscape is to be had, too, in the small things, in the billions of tiny details and individual items which make up the overall scene, in the minute patterns within the bigger design: the varied colours and shapes of lichens on a rock; the web of cracks on a frozen puddle; an air-born seed dancing in the wind; the way a current in the stream swirls around a fallen autumn leaf; gnarled tree roots paving a path; the grain on wood and rock; the microcosm of a rain-filled hollow in a fallen tree trunk; the patterns of different kinds of bark; a bee collecting pollen in a flower; swan's down drifting on the tide; the structure of a blade of grass. There is no end to the tiny miracles all around. The only limit is my own knowledge and powers of observation.

My final quality or ingredient is unity and harmony. Landscape beauty is more than a collection of disparate features. It is a result of them coming together as a unified whole that is greater than the sum of its parts.

Over the years I have noticed that the majority of my most deeply felt experiences of landscape beauty have three factors in common. The first of these is that the beauty was often ephemeral. These special moments have been exactly that – specific occasions, some of them never to be repeated: a particular moment created by the weather conditions, the clouds, the quality of light, the state of the tide, or the season of the year. In winter, for instance, even fairly unassuming places take on a purity, a virginal, ethereal quality. Mountains that were commoners in autumn become, in winter, magnificently crowned kings and queens. I recall one walk in the Great Forest of Ard where, after a heavy snowfall overnight, every branch and twig was outlined with snow, transforming the forest into a magical wonderland. The next day the snow was gone. Many a stretch of coastline I have paddled at high tide in one direction, returning by the same route at low tide along a shoreline that had completely changed in character. And, between low and high tide is an ephemeral world which exists for about two hours in a thirteen-hour cycle; a world of dwindling ground, channels swiftly swelling, expanding green lagoons, swaying kelp forests fast fading to fathoms down. Toe Head isthmus in Harris, when under daisies in summer, can blaze like a snowfield, then minutes later flush pink as the cups close in response to a cloud and a sharpening wind. The Fruin Hills are not especially spectacular, although I have a great fondness for them. But at four o'clock one spring morning with a pink mist gently spilling over the ridge they were outstandingly beautiful.

My comments about the ephemeral nature of landscape beauty need to be qualified. The full, deep and complete beauty of a landscape lies not only in the moments when it appears at its best according to human evaluation, but in the totality of what it is; in its day by day, year by year existence; in its million moods, its seasonal cycles, its overlapping time-scales and its diverse but orchestrated rhythms. Some years ago I realised that my relationships with the landscapes I thought I knew were all superficial. My acquaintance with them had lasted a few hours, perhaps a weekend, a few weeks at at the most. Even for places I visited again and again my presence there amounted to a minute fraction of a full seasonal cycle, let alone of other, larger, cycles of birth, growth, life, death and decay. With this in mind, I have started visiting, as often as possible, the Ballevoulin Burn which flows through a secluded glen in the Fruin Hills, no more than fifteen minutes by car from my home. My aim has been to observe the burn and its glen in all its moods, in every season and all times of day and night, in flood and in drought or in the grip of ice, in every type of weather and quality of light. Only now am I developing a proper appreciation of this unpretentious glen. Even on a dull, grey day I feel the beauty of it, for everything in that glen and every moment of its existence is part of a grander plan. That grey day may be just a toe-tap in the great dance of nature, a mere crotchet in the music of the universe, but it is enough, more than enough to fill me with wonder.

The second factor common to many of my own personal sweet especial scenes is that they often happen at the margins, the edges and the boundaries between one thing an another. I mean, for instance, the exciting zone where land and sea abut; the flora and fauna of river banks; the borders between day and night, abode of sunsets, twilight and the dawning of a new day; the fronts where weather systems clash, stirring the skies into riotous, hooligan behaviour; the Scottish mountains, lying as they do, on the boundaries between the tamed and the wild; or the Outer Hebrides, the islands on the edge of the sea, with their other-world atmosphere and the feeling they emanate that just over the horizon is Tir Nan Og, Land of the Ever-Young.

The Inuit used to navigate parts of the Greenland coast by

tasting the water. They knew that its salinity varied according to the proximity of river mouths and melting glaciers. In our own home waters, it is possible in thick mist to steer towards the Bass Rock, with its huge colony of gannets, without a compass. First you smell it, then you hear it and only at the last do you see it – all of which is by way of introducing the third factor common to my most enjoyable and deeply felt wilderness experiences. They have involved all five senses, and maybe other senses too.

In the context of landscape appreciation, hearing, smell, taste and touch are less frequently mentioned than seeing, but without their exercise a full appreciation must surely be incomplete. These four senses cannot be experienced from paintings or photographs, from distant viewpoints, or from a cruise liner's observation lounge. One needs to be there, in the landscape, involved with it. The landscape has a voice. It shouts, it sings, it murmurs, it whispers: High winds through a forest canopy have a summer sound and a winter sound and each species of tree its own dialect. The babble and chatter of a burn; the roar of a waterfall; the grunting cough of rutting stags echoing through high glens; thunder reverberating from cliff to cliff; a lark singing or the eerie cry of the Manx shearwater; waves lapping gently on a shore; the crash of surf on shifting shingle; the bass booming of a sea cave – listen to the land, listen to the sea.

One summer outing, which made a strong impression on me, took place in lowland farming country and involved, above all others, the sense of smell. My companion and I had decided to follow the course of the River Endrick, walking along its banks from where it flows into Loch Lomond to its source in the Gargunnock Hills. After a rather unpromising few hours bashing through nettles and clumps of bracken, evading brambles and climbing barbed-wire fences, we came upon a rolling meadow richly carpeted with flowers. The sheer extravagance of variety, the generosity of colour, the profusion and prodigality of perfumes was overwhelming – cornflowers, cowslips, buttercups, thistles, white campion, birdsfoot trefoil, lady's bedstraw, yarrow, meadowsweet, ox-eye daisies, cuckooflowers and many others I could not immediately identify – their combined scent so heady that in our ecstasy we could readily believe we had been granted a foretaste of Paradise. Curiously, in writing about the sense of smell, I have used the word 'foretaste.' But taste and smell do complement each other. In a mid-summer forest so rich is the aroma from wild garlic, seeping resins, leaf mould, the sweet greenness of ferns and blends of bosky scents that I can almost taste it. To pick wild berries and fungi, to slake a thirst at a mountain spring, or cook tickled trout over a driftwood fire is truly to internalise the land's natural beauty and make it part of me. 'Take, eat, this is my body.'[5]

I enjoy the roughness of bark and the heft of a hard, dry cone in the hand. Nowhere have I delighted in the texture of the land more than in the Cuillin of Skye. The coarse, crystalline gabbro provides so much friction that I have been able to saunter, hands in pockets, up steep-angled slabs which, anywhere else, would test an expert climber. Robert Macfarlane has interesting things to say about the pleasures of barefoot walking,[6] about the vast amount of information the soles of our feet can convey to us regarding the nature of the surfaces on which we tread, their textures, temperature and much else besides. Like most people, I have revelled in the feel of ribbed and rippled sands and the caress of warm smooth rock beneath unshod feet, the tickle of springy turf and the satisfying squelch of mud between the toes, and felt contact with the land become more intimate.

As I suspected, a full definition of landscape beauty remains elusive. Nor have my few examples done justice to the infinite wonder of it all. I do know, though, that landscapes, like human beings, are beautiful for reasons well beyond their physical attributes. And I am in no doubt when I am in the presence of that sweet especial scene. I do not need to think about it or analyse it: that haiku moment, that intake of breath and quickening of the heart; feelings of joy, pleasure, happiness, exhilaration, awe and wonder; the engagement of all my faculties and total absorption of the mind; emotional and spiritual renewal and a sense of touching the sublime, of connecting with something greater than myself. And it is not something outside of us, but internal. As Mary Austin wrote: 'Man is not himself only, he is all that he sees; all that flows to him from a thousand sources. He is the land, the lift of its mountain lines, the reach of its valleys.[7]

NOTES

The title of this essay is taken from 'The Land of Little Rain' by Mary Austin: 'Man is not himself only/ He is all that he sees/ All that flows from a thousand sources/ He is the land, the lift of its mountains, the reach of its valleys.' Mary Hunter Austin (1868-1934)was one of the early nature wirers of the American Southwest.

1. Measured at high tide. This figure represents 70% of the total UK coastline.

2. Robert Lambert: 'Contested Mountains: Nature, Development and Environment in the Cairngorms Region of Scotland 1880-1989'.

3. I am indebted to an excellent article 'Landscape Perception and Inhabiting Vision' by Noel Hefell for deepening my understanding of this point.

4 Joe Cornish, *First Light: A Landscape Photographer's Art* (Argentum, 2002).

5 Matthew 26.26

6 Robert Macfarlane, *The Old Ways: A Journey on Foot* (Hamish Hamilton, 2012).

7 Quoted from *The Land of Little Rain* (1903) by the American writer, Mary Austin (1868-1934).

A KIND OF HOMECOMING

I was thankful for the tiny cabin which sheltered me from the spray as the chartered motor-boat plunged and butted into the waves. We were heading for the Monach Isles, a group of small, low-lying islands, five miles off the west coast of North Uist. For over a thousand years they were inhabited; and a nunnery and a monastery were built there in the thirteenth century. In the late 1800s the population of crofters and fishing folk began to decline. The Monach Isles used to have a school, a post office and a lighthouse. However, by the start of World War Two, only a few people, including the lighthouse keeper and his family, still lived there. In 1942 the lighthouse was abandoned; and in 1947, the islands became uninhabited when the last remaining family took fright and left after a particularly severe storm.

Thirty-five years ago, accompanied by my friend John, I had made the crossing to the Monach Islands in a kayak. We had done it in much the same sea conditions as now. It was a crossing I was no longer capable of undertaking by kayak, for the wheel of life revolves and all living things have their points of return and built-in homecomings.

All those years ago John and I had set off into the wide expanses of the ocean, our low-lying destination below the horizon, nothing ahead but Atlantic and more Atlantic and rolling slate-blue downs, ploughed and furrowed by a westerly force five wind. After an hour of paddling a black needle pricked the skyline – the lighthouse on Shillay, one of the smaller of the five Monach islands. The needle grew taller, but still no land was visible. Then, each time we rose on a wave, a faint, blurred horizontal line was discernible, which slowly focused and became separate islands. Messages reached us on the wind, clover-scented messages, the flower-sweet breath of the Monach Isles. Drawing closer, we passed a series of sandy bays from which whole colonies of Atlantic Grey Seals emerged, groups of thirty or forty, to surround us and escort us past their territory. We landed on Ceann Ear, the biggest of the islands, an island of machair and meadowland, a magical carpet of flowers unrolled on an empty sea. We looked back to 'The Long Isle' we'd left behind – the chain of Lewis, Harris, North Uist, South Uist and Barra forming a continuous misty line. That night the seals were singing, a sound not unlike a dog keening, not unlike the wind or the singing sands, but more musical, more evocative.

The motor-boat bumped alongside a small wooden jetty. Would Ceann Ear be as I remembered it? It was. Here again were the silver strands, the rippling Marram grass, the scent of the flowers mingling with the scent of the sea, butterflies flitting over the machair. In that moment I knew two things to be true: If you leave your heart in a place, if part of you stayed behind, then to return is a homecoming. And if you respond to that deep psychological need for the wilderness and wildness of our origins, that, too, is a homecoming.

TIME OUT IN SHETLAND

Four of us launch our kayaks into thick mist. We are reaching turning points in our lives. We paddle in silence, our thoughts elsewhere.

the mainland fades
but the island ahead still
has not appeared

Away from the shore, a quiet swell is rolling up the sound. But on the margins, where the North Atlantic finally meets land, even gentle swells explode on outlying rocks, seething and foaming between the skerries.

A headland, then cliffs and pointed stacks loom through the mist. We wind through narrow, echoing canyons, never knowing what lies ahead. As we pass under a low arch the sun breaks through.

seen through clear green sea
darting fish, or the shadows
of skimming gulls?

Landing, we share our food and our feelings of uncertainty.

sandy cliff-girt beach –
pounded shells, bones, stone and glass
made one by the sea.

THE REALMS OF NIGHT

My fascination with the realms of night goes back a long way. Age six: my father meeting my mother, brother and self off the boat at Bombay, driving us through the night across the Deccan Plateau – the blazing red eyes of packs of jackals caught in the cars headlights, the luminous orbs of the buffalo, the singing of frogs that filled the soft scented air, the distant flicker of lightening, columns of illuminated dust raised by a passing truck, a huge orange sun sliding slowly above the horizon. Age thirteen: on my first youthful camping trips with friends, becoming aware, in a way one never does indoors, of sunsets, starry nights, the travelling moon and the calls of nocturnal animals. Age seventeen: at the tiller of Grakle, my father's ketch, crossing from Dartmouth to Cherbourg at two o'clock in the morning, the phosphorescence on the crests of the waves, stars falling across the sky, the pool of light from the compass-well like an oasis in the darkness. As a student at Cambridge: climbing the ancient buildings at night – shinning up drainpipes or ornately carved and gargoyle facades, traversing steeply tiled roofs with the silent streets below, leaping across gaps between one building and another (one leap was best not done sober, so it was thought, or you hesitated fatally at the crucial moment), lying beneath the big clock on the college tower, a second moon in the sky, as it boomed out the midnight hour.

There have been climbs in the Alps which started at three or four in the morning to cross a glacier before snow bridges over deep crevasses softened in the sun and collapsed under our weight, usually the first hour roped together passes in silence, breath hissing into the crisp air, crampons crunching across moon-blue ice, metal axes ringing, the high peaks catching the first rays of the sun. And there was the moonlight ascent of Ben Ime with Martin about which I have written earlier in this collection.

A Greenland summer offers an entirely different sort of night adventure, if you can call it night in a land where the sun doesn't set for several months. We would some-times paddle until midnight and eat our 'evening' meal at one or two in the morning, still able to see with comparative ease. The following is an extract from my book *Fallen Pieces of the Moon* about a short walk at three o'clock of an Arctic morning:

I walked a little way up the slope and sat in the springy scrub. A light breeze had sprung up again: just the right amount to keep the mosquitoes and other bugs at bay. Clouds, like slowly drifting windflowers, bloomed in shades of pink. To the east the higher snow slopes blushed at the touch of the low lying sun and steep rock faces glowed like molten lava as though, any moment, the would pour in rivers of scarlet and gold into a sea bejewelled with floating rubies.

Kayaking at night contains pleasures not found by day. I recall an island campsite in a tree-ringed glade carpeted with pine needles; green-flamed fir cones sparking in the fire. Archie and I decided on a moonlight paddle. As we passed dark islands, birds stirred and murmured. The sweet smell of bog myrtle filled the night air as we slid silently down a silver highway In front of us a stag swam from one island to another, its antlers silhouetted against the stars. .

Once, after a long day paddling from Helensburgh down Loch Long, I found myself returning in the dark. Greenock, Gourock and Dunoon shimmered in the distance and the Cloch Point Lighthouse blinked steadily. I nosed into a small inlet for a rest and thankfully eased myself out of the narrow cockpit. Surrounded by stranded tree trunks which had been stripped and smoothed by the sea until they resembled moon-bathing beasts from outer space, I toasted my sandwiches over a driftwood fire. The sea was restless beyond the little bay and a spread of dark wings hid a new-hatched moon. On rounding a point I was greeted by a new galaxy of lights – a bright cluster that was the oil rig. I knew this home stretch so well, yet I was confused. Lights were not where they should be. Was it banks of mist, or unseen headlands breaking the expected pattern? And which was reflection and which was not? Something huge and monstrous broke the surface, flailing the water and screeching horribly. I nearly capsized from sheer fright. A panic of wings churned the water and flapped heavily into the air – gulls. They had been resting on a sandbank I'd failed to see.

Two other night paddles embedded in my mind were both unplanned. The first was when, on the way to Oban, a wheel came off the trailer. By the time it was fixed it was pretty late although still light since it was close to midsummer. On an impulse, Ian and I decided not to bother putting up the tent, but simply to launch and paddle round Kerrera, down the outside and back up the inner passage. This was the kind of trip one does 'once in a blue moon'. So it was fitting that the next full moon, although still a week away, was indeed a blue moon – which is defined as being either the second full moon in one month, or the third full moon in a (three month) season which contains four full moons. The blazing sky, the long lingering twilight shot with gradually bruising clouds, the silhouettes of the Mull mountains against an orange glow and the long vista, in the simmer dim, down the Firth of Lorn with the with the Garvellachs, Colonsay and Jura clearly visible, and the crackling fire when we stopped in the darkest hour, then skimming through the softly approaching dawn in a kayak named Dawn Treader – these things are now a part of me.

The second was on Loch Morar. The day had been made memorable by a glorious rainbow which arched the loch and the roaring of stags, echoing in the high glens on either side of us. Later though, it clouded over and began to drizzle. The five of us beached our kayaks at the head of the loch quite late in the day only to find that the bothy we had planned to use was locked barred. We had no tents with us and it was cold, damp evening. Sleeping out in the open was not an inviting prospect. With night closing in on us we decided to paddle back to where we had left the cars, It was a murky, overcast night. Fortunately Loch Morar has very few powered boats on it likely to run us down in the dark. Although it is not mandatory in UK waters for kayaks to carry navigation lights (red lights on port side, green lights on starboard side, white lights fore and aft), and although we had not foreseen this turn of events, most of us could muster a strobe light for permanently stowed in our bags. Between us we could muster a strobe light for switching on if something big and menacing was bearing down on us, three or four red lights for clipping to the stern or the back of a lifejacket, the same number of headlamps for use when reading a map or doing something fiddly, and a couple of powerful spotlight torches for picking out hazards and potential landing places; and all of us had strips of reflective tape on our presence – unlike a red flare, a white flare is not a distress signal and hopefully will not trigger a rescue operation. Even with this equipment it was all too easy to lose touch with each other and we resorted to continually shouting out a roll call of our names: 'Robin here!' 'Michael here!' Loch Morar is quite shallow in places, with sharpish rocks inches beneath the surface or lurking just high enough to be mistaken for a black lump of water. A breeze had sprung up, causing waves to swirl around the protruding rocks, sometimes warning us of their presence, sometimes not.

When the shallows became too dangerous we would move out into the middle of the loch. In the dark, with the shores invisible, I was seized by a strong sense of the inky black depths beneath me. Loch Morar, at over 1,000 feet deep, is the deepest loch in Scotland, deeper than Loch ness, and deeper than the sea for 150 miles out into the Atlantic until the edge of the shelf is reached beyond St Kilda. If ever there was a night for encountering Morag, the resident monster, this was it.

Out in the middle it was difficult to see where we were in relation to the shore or to keep track of our progress. Anxious not to pass our parked cars without knowing it, we moved closer to the shore again. I read somewhere that the retina in our eyes which best translate low-level light into nerve impulses are on the edges of our pupils. We therefore see objects better at night if we look 5 to 20 degrees away from them. I think, possibly, we do this slight turning of the head back and forth when peering into the dark instinctively. My optician, on the other hand, says this is rubbish. Her exact words were: 'In practical terms, it doesn't make a blind bit of difference!'

I kept losing sight of the others, or narrowly missing things that jumped out of the gloom without warning. Colin, who seemed to have catlike vision, internal radar and several extra senses led the way. But for him I would have rammed into the almost invisible obstacles several times over – jagged things which stuck out of the water like a monster's spine. In the dark, one stretch of tree-lined shore looked much like another, and the same went for beaches, inlets and just about everything else. Passages between islands so easily navigated by day became nightmares of uncertainty amongst the nearby undergrowth. Finally, Colin's torch picked out a beach and beyond it our parked cars. I don't know whether it was the long day paddling down the length of Loch Morar and back again, or the stress of concentrating so hard in the darkness, but we were all strangely disoriented when we got out of our kayaks, staggering about the road, unable to walk a straight line. No, we weren't drunk, except with relief and with deep satisfaction that we had turned what could have been a dismal ending to the day into a memorable experience.

When we draw the curtains and turn on the lights we banish night from our man-made world. Simply stepping outside may not be enough, for urban light pollution has so dimmed the heavens that those of us living in cities barely register the awe and beauty of the night sky. But offshore or in the mountains exploring the realms of night can be richly rewarding There have been so many magic moments when other senses are alerted and when familiar places become new and exciting and utterly transformed.

THREE SHORT ESSAYS CLOSE TO HOME

Photographing the lovage

Growing in a shaded corner of my garden is an eight-foot clump of lovage – a stout, umbelliferous plant, a hardy perennial herb which belongs to the same family as fennel, dill, carrots, parsley and parsnips. It has ribbed and hollow stems, compound leaves and flowers that offer their yellow and white umbels to the sky. Lovage is intriguingly versatile. Its roots, leaves, seeds and stems all have medicinal and culinary uses.

I am in the habit of wandering in my garden, camera in hand, trying to be open and receptive, ready for something to find me. Today it was the lovage. What held my attention was the engineering precision of the plant; its amazing architecture and structural design; the subtlety of light falling on different surfaces; the hinted order behind the apparent chaos of foliage.

In ancient China, so the story goes, an apprentice asked the great master, Wang Fu, to teach him to paint bamboo. Wang Fu forbade him to touch his brushes. Instead, he must meditate in front of the bamboo until he and the bamboo became as one; until he was the bamboo. Only then could he paint it. Well, I can't claim that it was quite the same between me and the lovage, but for ten minutes I did stand in front of it, walk around it, peer into it and view it from a crouch and from on tiptoe, trying to connect with it as it swayed gently in the wind.

There is something inherently aggressive about much of Western photography. We talk about 'capturing' a subject, or 'taking' it; or even 'shooting; it. What I strive for is to receive an image rather than take it; to regard it as gift. Photographing the lovage was an act of praise, a prayer. Looking at it and really seeing it was a precious moment of mindfulness in which I glimpsed the extraordinary in the ordinary.

Picking wild raspberries

Wild the raspberries may be, but they are well established in my garden. They occupy a strip about fifty feet long and ten feet wide, bordered on one side by a high stone wall and by a grassy area on the other. To call the latter a lawn would be sheer flattery. At first strawberries grew along that strip by the wall, then a variety of heathers was planted. These succumbed to an invasion of blackberry bushes, which held sway for several years before the raspberries made a bid for supremacy and won. A milder winter, a wetter summer, more salt spray off the sea than usual, a virus that attacked one species but not another, some shift in the make-up of the garden's insect population – any of these, or other variables, could have tipped the balance in their favour.

The crowns and roots of raspberry plants are perennial, but individual canes live two years. They grow during the first summer, bear fruit in the second summer and then die shortly afterwards. You will gather that I am not a fanatical eradicator of unplanned plants. My attitude to gardening is laissez faire. Would-be writers complain that they don't have the time to write. I tell them there is no such thing as not having time, only having different priorities. And I offer my neglected garden as an example of what I mean. But, even if I did give more time to gardening, I would still choose to have a garden that was on the wild side. There has always been an unresolved tension in gardening between the extent to which we feel the garden belongs to nature and the extent to which we feel it belongs to us; whether it is an expression of nature or of human artistic aspirations. It is a matter of how much domination and control over our gardens we want. There are no straight lines in nature. I don't feel comfortable in symmetrical gardens where everything is geometrically arranged and with plants in regimented rows. Even worse (in my opinion) are the hedges and bushes tamed, trimmed and trained into shapes far removed from their natural form. I am in agreement with the pioneer of wild gardens, William Robinson (1838-1935), who held that it was Nature who was the supreme artist, and the gardener only the assistant. He believed in trusting Nature and staying true to her guidance.

I am not sure what William Robinson thought about weeds. I joke that my garden is a British weed sanctuary. Most weeds are beautiful if you look at them in a positive way. A weed, after all, is only an unwanted plant, a plant out of place. The wording on the boxes of weed-killer in my local garden centre is the language of the police state and the holocaust: control, targeted, selective, Kill, poison, instant death, eradicate, gone for good. I prefer peaceful co-existence.

Thoughts such as these wander through my mind as I pick the raspberries. The advice most often given to writers about how to stimulate their creativity is, 'Go for a walk.' Fruit-picking has much the same effect. The repetitive activity allows the mind to wander and coaxes it down unexplored paths. This mini-raspberry forest is full of metaphors for life. The way, for instance, that the biggest and most luscious fruit are just out of reach or guarded by the fiercest thorns; how, in order to fulfil their role in life, the raspberries must signal their presence and readiness to the world; the ease with which the fruit is picked when the time is

Right, no force necessary; or how there is often a surprisingly rich haul when you look on the underside of the plant, when you peer into the darkest thicket, or crouch low. Even the slightest shift in the angle at which I look at the canes brings new perspectives and reveals fruit I would not otherwise have seen. The act of picking is rather like tai chi – I move slowly and deliberately to avoid being scratched. I stretch up, bend down, reach forward and sideways – slowly, so as not to break the canes or knock the ripe fruit to the ground. Just occasionally, when my breathing synchronises with my movements, I feel that there is no separation between the garden and the gardener.

Amongst the many things these wild raspberries have taught me is patience. They will mature and ripen when they are ready and not before. Unlike many other soft fruits they don't continue to ripen once they are picked. I have learned to wait, to respect their natural rhythm.

Sometimes, instead of dropping a raspberry into the bowl, I pop it into my mouth. I am told that ethyl formate which gives raspberries their flavour is found in the clouds of gas and cosmic dust that drift through the heavens millions of light years away. Does outer space taste of raspberries? Raspberries are a way into my inner space, too. When fully grown some of the canes are above my head. They enclose me, becoming a little oasis of peace and solitude. These wild raspberries are rich in vitamins and antioxidants good for my bodily health; and picking them in this quiet corner of my garden is a calming, beneficial act of meditation.

The old tree trunk on the shore

On Christmas Eve I went for a walk along the shore at Helensburgh. Thick mist cocooned me in a still, silent world of hinted shapes. Next month would be my wife's eightieth birthday. we were both getting old.

About ten minutes along the shore I encountered an old friend – a tree trunk, nine or ten feet long, which had been tossed above the high-water mark in a storm. It had lain there for the last twelve years, gradually decaying. Its bark, year by year, had peeled away, exposing the grain of the wood. Knots, conks and cankers caused eddies and counter-currents in the flow. Sand-blasted, frost-bitten, corded, the grain bar-coded message of metamorphosis.

Beetles, millipedes, mites and worms had catacombed and labyrinthed the wood. In places it had been burned, adding dark and different textures. Slime molds, jelly-rot fungi, algae and other mucilaginous forms inhabited its surface in concentric circles, geometric shapes and magical mandalas. Colonies of colour patterned the trunk in shades of purple, green, orange, cream and brown. Lit by the low winter sun and moistened by the mist, the trunk glistened, its magnificence magnified and enhanced.

Holding my camera in gnarled, brown-blotched hands and bending on stiff knees to attain the best angles, I recorded life emerging from death and beauty born of decay.

A WALK UP DUBH EAS BURN

The Dubh Eas Burn flows through Gleann nan Caorann in an easterly direction off the southern flanks of Ben Oss into the River Falloch which soon afterwards enters the northern end of Loch Lomond. Dubh Eas is Gaelic for black waterfall and Caorann means rowan tree or mountain ash. One June day I decided to follow the burn up from where it joins the River Falloch to near its source. I was on my own which meant I could take as many photographs as I liked and linger over a shot for as long as I wanted without putting others in a fret. Not that such self-denial on my part has been appreciated by my companions who claim to have noted a correlation between my spotting a must-take shot and my need of a rest.

It hadn't rained for about ten days and the water-level in the burn was low. I was able to walk up the course of the burn, hopping from boulder to boulder. At this point it was at its widest and slowest, about fifty feet from bank to bank, a series of quiet pools linked by boulders, shingle strands and a gently rippling flow. This whole lower section of the burn was overhung by large oaks that formed a leafy tunnel, through which filtered a greeny-yellow light that was reflected in the pools. All the time, the banks on either side were getting higher, so that I was now in a shaded gorge.

I was halted by a natural dam. Whole trees and boulders, carried downstream at those times when the burn was in full spate, had jammed at a narrowing of the burn's course. The dead trees, now stripped of bark, pale and chorded, resembled strange monsters emerged from the depths of the lake beyond. The lake, or mabybe it was a large pond, was enclosed by black cliffs. At the far end, a waterfall appeared out of the thick woodland to plunge thirty feet, sending ripples over the placid water below. This is the black waterfall from which the

Dubh Eas Burn gets its name.

The cliffs were too steep and slippery to climb. I back-tracked and prepared to exit the gorge by an easier route. Directly above me the Glen Falloch Railway Viaduct carried the West Highland Line across the gorge, its lattice of iron girders framed against the sky. Built in 1894, it crosses the gorge in one 118 foot span; and is only a few feet less in height than the famous Forth Rail Bridge.

Using hand and footholds offered by trees that clung to the slope I gained the narrow path which ran along the top of the gorge, passed the waterfall and then kept parallel to the burn. Despite the dry spell, the burn made a splendid show of cascading down down its steep, rocky course. Through stands of sliver birch, and rowans, not yet in berry, I glimpsed its sliding, swirling, foaming rush to join the Falloch; and heard, sometimes loud, sometimes faint, its insistant but companionable voice.

The trees gave way to moorland and the morning to a pleasant sunny afternoon with cumulus clouds grazing a blue sky. The gradient eased off and the flow of the burn once more became gentle. I think here, in its upper reaches, the burn must have been flowing over a strata of different, more porous rock, for the whole nature of the burn changed. In front of me was a rock and water maze of intriguing complexity, a miniature Tolkienesque mountainscape of spires, knife-edged ridges, cwms and steep winding canyons. In places it was like standing on top of a dissected honeycomb. Maybe I was dreaming I was in a sculpture park crammed with abstract creations. Or had the Earth Gods invited me to their table? Caskets were filled with shiny mottled pebbles. Quartz chalices brimmed with sparkling liquid.

Over millions of years flowing water had sculpted the rock. Bowls, cups and hollows had been scraped smooth by swirling grit-laden currents and polished labyrinthine passages similarly fashioned. And the colours! The palest blues, pinks, honey hues and the full gamut of browns, enriched by graining, patterned by cracks, fissures and quartz veins and adorned by lichens in yellows, greys and shades of white. In stone nests lay stone clutches of song sparrow's, dove's and blackbird's eggs in all their spotted and speckled variety.

The Dubh Eass burn runs through, over, between these formations, sweeping around eroded curves, gushing through the mini-gorges, sliding in smooth runnels from rock pool to rock pool, or overflowing from one basin to another.

That June day I had chanced upon the burn in a perfect balance, poised between the water level being low enough to expose its visual treasures, and sufficiently high for there to be enough flow to play among these shapes, fill the bowls, wet the colours into life; for rock and water to offset each other and delight in each other's company.

THE ASCENT OF BEN GLAS

Ben Glas (meaning 'greenish-grey mountain' in Gaelic) lies on the eastern side of Glen Falloch at the point where the glen opens out to meet the north end of Loch Lomond. It is 654 metres high (2,145 feet and 8 inches) – not very high at all, in fact – and with grander neighbours in all directions. And yet it took Archie and me six attempts before we stood on the summit of this insignificant peak. Forty years ago I could have been up there in under two hours and descended in half that time, bounding down in big, soaring leaps with knees capable of absorbing the shock. But that was forty years ago. At the time of our first attempt, our combined age was 150 years. By the final attempt we had both passed eighty. Together, we could muster two coronary by-passes, a heart attack, a stent insertion, a titanium knee, two cases of angina, one case of prostate cancer, a host of minor age-related ailments and creaking joints and not enough hair between us to stuff a tennis ball. Not that either of us really thought of ourselves as old, even though the candles cost more than the cake and our wild oats had turned to all-bran. George Bernard Shaw once said: 'You don't stop playing because you're old; you become old when you stop playing.' We would both subscribe to that.

Six attempts at a mere pimple? I mean, this isn't the Himalayas I'm describing. Well, a prime consideration in this saga was the nature of the terrain. No footpaths lead to the top. The walking was unremitting hard work over rough ground. We seemed to go against the grain of the country no matter from which direction we made our approach – up the side of a ridge, down the other side, over and over again. The area is a maze of hollows and hillocks, small cliffs, mini-gorges, swales, bogs, lochans, passes that lead nowhere and yet more ridges to ascend and descend. Although physical fitness – or the lack of it – was undoubtedly a major factor in our Ben Glas expeditions, a bigger factor was our mental approach. That is to say, neither of us felt it to be desperately important whether we got to the top or not. Gone were those testosterone fuelled days of youth when the mountains were a personal challenge, when there was something to prove and one's pride and self-image made turning back seem like a bitter defeat. Over the years, as we mellowed and matured (like all good wines should), as the hormone balance in our bodies shifted, we began to want not conquest, but connection. Conquest is about domination, putting a flag on the peak, naming a route, or earning bragging rights. Connection is about being part of the landscape, feeling a sense of unity and harmony with it. By this time we were devotees of the dérive. A dérive is an unplanned wander in which you respond creatively to whatever stimuli you encounter on the way. Our enjoyment lay in the journey rather than in reaching the destination. Our choice of where we went was determined more by the desire to encounter natural beauty in all its forms than by the challenge it presented or the extent to which it would test our manhood. We walked slowly not only because we were too decrepit to do otherwise, but also the better to observe and absorb our surroundings. Such concerns as keeping to a schedule, putting up a fast time, or of doing it quicker than suggested in some guide book were no longer ours. Some lines from the poem, 'The Messenger', by Mary Oliver come to mind:

> Let me keep my mind on what matters, which is my work,
> Which is mostly standing still and learning to be astonished.

That is the real goal for me. Not the distant peak, but being astonished along the way, experiencing the world around me with all my senses as if for the first time. We go slowly, too, because I take a lot of photographs.

Our first outing towards Ben Glas was on a bright autumn day. We parked at the old drovers' inn and walked up the steep, narrow track beside the Ben Glas Burn which tumbles down the hillside in churning chutes, through roaring gorges and over a succession of falls, of which the 300 foot Eagle Falls is the most spectacular. Above this we encountered barren moorland, boggy with recent rain. We followed the burn on a muddy, clinging, energy-sucking track until it petered out and we took to the mountainside. A scramble up a stony gully brought us to a minor top. From below it had looked like the start of a ridge which might take us most of the way. Instead, we gazed upon a confusing jumble of tops, like steep waves in a storm, their crests and troughs barring the way to our goal. Yes, we had consulted the map, but when the ground is as broken as this, it doesn't offer much help.

Our slight disappointment was more than compensated for by the view. To the south we could see down the length of Loch Lomond, its twenty-two miles glinting in the sun and Ben Lomond, the most southerly 3,000 foot mountain in Scotland, flying a cloud banner. To the west were the wooded flanks of Gleann nan Caorann (Glen of the Rowan Tree), still decked in autumn colours. A large percentage of these mixed woodlands are birch and the increasingly rare Atlantic oak, with scattered remnants of the ancient Caledonian pine forest. Spanning Gleann nan Caorann was the Glen Falloch viaduct, opened in 1894 and still in use by the West Highland Railway. Northwards, broad and green, was Glen Falloch, its silver river uncoiling from the Grampian Mountains.

Two hours later, and after a lot of effort, we stood on the shores of Lochan a'Chaisteil (The Little Loch of the Castle). Enfolded and sheltered, its round surface was like a mirror, reflecting, in perfect detail, the cliff which rose sheer from the water to the summit of Ben Glas. The sun was low in the sky, combining with the dead autumn grass and dry bracken to cast a red glow over everything. We had run out of energy. That last push to the top, we knew, was going to be too much for us. We had run out of time, too. The shortening days meant that, should we take another hour to get there, we would be stumbling down difficult terrain in the dark.

We made a second excursion that winter. The River Falloch gushed between ice-embossed boulders, slid darkly beneath translucent slabs, then burst out again, swirling chunks of snow and ice downstream. The Eagle Falls were frozen from top to bottom, draped in thick ropes and sheets of ice. Ben Lui was robed in snow from base to summit, its huge white corrie catching the sun. I took a great many photographs that day. Possibly because of this, and because the sun was setting at half past three in the afternoon, we again ran out of time.

'We shall return!' proclaimed Archie, with all the conviction of General Douglas MacArthur.

At this point I was diagnosed with prostate cancer and underwent an intensive course of radiotherapy. The treatment was tiring and weakening, so were the side-effects which had me running to the loo every thirty minutes or so, twenty-four hours of the day, for the next six months. My walks got shorter and shorter, flatter and flatter. Ben Glas became a motivation to get fit again, something to aim at, a dream to hold onto through the rough patch. Soon after the radiography ended I spent two weeks on a cruise ship as a cruise lecturer. Every day I made a point of walking up the stairs from Deck Two to Deck Ten: eight flights of twenty steps, each step a vertical six inches. Doing this twenty-seven times would be roughly the equivalent of ascending Ben Glas. It wasn't looking good because it took me the full two weeks to complete the quota. Back in Helensburgh the number of lengths I swam in the municipal pool gradually increased and the walks began to lengthen. There came a moment when Archie and I decided it was time for a bigger day out, a sort of dress-rehearsal for Ben Glas. We chose Dumgoyne, a volcanic plug near Killearn, 700 feet lower than Ben Glas and with a path all the way to the top, but with some fairly steep bits in places. Half way up the path we decided it was too boring and headed for a gully which promised a bit more interest. It turned out to be rather too interesting. I completely exhausted myself scrambling up wet and slippery rocks. I arrived at the top of the gully and collapsed. Every time I tried to stand up my rubber legs buckled beneath me. I lay there, hardly able to move. Archie wrapped me in a plastic sheet and phoned for help. About forty minutes later a helicopter arrived, lifted me off the hillside and took me to a hospital in Glasgow. After a check up, a good rest and a cup of tea, the doctor said I was fine. I had simply tried to do too much too soon. He added that it gladdened him to see people of my age still on the hills and that, no way should I consider stopping. I'm still taking a lot of ribbing about that incident. Me, a former outdoor activities instructor, who gave lectures on mountain safety, having to be rescued! Anyway, two weeks later we returned to Dumgoyne and walked up it without difficulty. But I had to admit I wasn't ready for Ben Glas.

Finally, more than a year after the radiography ended, engagements with Ben Glas resumed. After half an hour of going up a steep slope, wading through knee-deep snow with a heavy pack on my back, I suddenly felt very ill. I was having an attack of angina, possibly even a heart attack. I applied my GTN spray under the tongue, rested and, with Archie carrying my pack, went very slowly down again. On reaching the path (a section of the West Highland Way) we took a slightly longer route to the main road because it was downhill. Archie walked back to the parked car from there. By the time he returned with the car, the sun was setting, giving the snow-clad peaks a rosy tint and a golden sheen to the ice-bound burn.

Later that winter, in a white-shrouded landscape, we got close to the summit. We were confident of success. A sudden drop in temperature and an icy wind changed everything. It became very, very cold – dangerously cold. Higher up it would be even colder. We retreated.

Yet another retreat was caused by Archie and I losing each other. Earlier in the day we had been looking down on cloud-filled valleys, with wispy tendrils, here and there, drifting upwards. We reached the zone of chaos. Archie chose to climb a small rocky bluff; I chose to go round the side of it, expecting to be reunited with him at the top. I didn't see him again for several hours. I searched the rocky maze, calling out, unsure whether he was ahead of me or behind. I pushed on, thinking we were bound to meet up at Lochan a'Chaisteil. But he wasn't there. Was he lying injured somewhere? We both had mobile phones with us, but the person to person service did not work in these hills, only emergency services. I phoned Mountain Rescue and told them about Archie, who was over eighty and might be in trouble. 'Ah!' said the voice at the other end. 'Archie has just phoned to say that he's worried about his elderly friend who might be in trouble.'

'Another fine mess you've got me into,' Archie said when we were finally reunited.

We had tried from the south, from the east and from the west. Now, probably fitter than we had been for quite some time, we were going to try from the north. The plan was to follow the Allt a'Chuillin (the stream of the holly groves), one of the River Falloch's larger tributaries, until we were level with a saddle on the ridge that lead from Ben Glas to the much higher Beinn Chabhair (Hawk Mountain). The latter we had climbed several times in the past, but today our sights were set on its lowly satellite. It was May. The ash, alder, rowan and willow that lined the burn were putting out fresh green leaves. The burn was in full spate from meltwater off the higher slopes, providing displays of crashing energy and bubbling ebullience. The corrie gradually opened out to broader vistas under a wide open, ever-changing sky. The hours went by, the rest-stops became more frequent. Descending into one of the many hollows, Archie took a tumble, rolling several feet down stony ground. Visions of yet another rescue flashed through my mind. He stood up, insisting he was alright and we plodded on at our tortoise pace. 'Surely this is the last ridge?' we both thought – several times. 'Surely we will see the lochan below us and the summit nearby when we top this rise?' Then, at last, there they were.

'We knocked the bastard off!' I said, trying to sound like the

New Zealander, Edmund Hillary.

Despite my claim that conquering peaks is no longer of importance to me, I was overjoyed to be standing on Ben Glas's rocky summit. The sense of achievement was every bit as great as doing a Munro in hard winter conditions, as attaining an Alpine peak, or on reaching Annapurna Base Camp in the Himalayas.

In our various attempts we had gained the kind of intimacy with a mountain granted only to those who experience it in all seasons and conditions and who have seen it from every angle. Ben Glas taught me not just to accept that ageing brings limitations, but to see that it offers new gifts. Until I was forced to slow down I never realised I was walking past a million natural miracles without noticing. I discovered the difference between seeing as opposed to merely looking. Aided by my camera lens, which focused my attention, I found the extraordinary in the ordinary. I found beauty in small things I would have hurried by in my youth: lichen patterns on a boulder; blades of grass encased in ice; the swirl and flow of water in a burn; the structure of plants, or the grain of eroded rock. I was given the beginnings of an awareness that the whole is in every part and that tiny things and subtle details are pathways to a richer, broader consciousness.

My explorations of this humble hill showed me that old age itself is something to be explored, something in which there are surprises and unexpected gifts. Our autumn and winter excursions on Ben Glas had been every bit as beautiful, in their own ways, as had been those of spring and summer. It could be true also, I realised, of the seasons of my life. On the winter days on Ben Glas the last downhill stretch before reaching the car was invariably done in the dark. Only then did we see what was invisible by day: the sky filled with stars.

NEAR IS THE NEW FAR

As I get older I tend not to drive as far as I used to before beginning a hillwalk or launching my kayak. A long drive was worth it when a typical day in the mountains or on the water lasted seven or eight hours and occasionally went into double figures. Now, at age eighty-three, I am pleased with myself if I manage three or four hours. Since my rule has always been not to spend more time driving there and back than I spend on the actual activity, the distance I am prepared to travel is becoming shorter and shorter.

These days I visit the places I overlooked and drove past on my way to the bigger mountains, the more challenging waters and the remoter parts of Scotland. And very rewarding it has been. However, what I want to write about here are the places which are really near, places not more than two or three minutes from my back door, five minutes at the most. That is to say, I am going to write here about our garden and the sea shore beyond it.

A high stone wall marks the garden's western boundary. Constructed of sandstone blocks held together by mortar, it was built in 1850, at the same time as the house. Since then it has received only a minimum of repair. In places the mortar has disintegrated, leaving gaps between the stones – little crevices and caves, Bug Hotel and des res for minibeasts of all sorts. With a torch in one hand and a large magnifying glass in the other an hour can easily slip away as I become lost in another world.

The wall is cracked, pitted and eroded by salt winds and the frosts of 168 winters. I like to close my eyes and run my finger-tips over its uneven, abrasive surface, exploring its variety of gritty textures. Its Braille-like messages are 'eloquent to my hands.'[1] I encounter a miniature moss maze where circular grooves have been chiselled into the stone, for what purpose I do not know. The lichens feel rather like a thick coat of peeling paint, sometimes crusty and fibrous, sometimes powdery. Then my skin informs me I'm touching a lichen described as squamulose – one with small, leafy scales. Lichens cover about 6% of the Earth's land surface. They are certainly covering more than that on our wall. Lichens are not plants, but an organism that emerges from a partnership between fungi and algae. The fungi protect and house the algae; and the algae, through photosynthesis, provide food for the fungi. These miniature eco-systems are among the oldest living things on our planet. Opening my eyes I am treated to a visual feast of whites, greys, and orangey-yellows. The lichens' shapes are food for the imagination, too – archipelagos, mythical landscapes, coded messages from Mars, abstract paintings.

On the other side of the garden, in a corner between another wall and a boundary hedge, is a small pond. This was dug about twelve years ago by my wife and me for the benefit of the wild mallard ducks which fly in most mornings. Here, in this protected space, overhung by the branches of a lime tree, the ducklings can safely swim, watched over by their mother. Anywhere else in the garden or on the shore crows and seagulls pick them off. Watching the ducks gives immense pleasure, so does watching the pond itself. Although we change the water in the pond regularly, it doesn't take long in summer and autumn for it to develop a greenish hue and for leaves, flowers and petals to fall into it. They drift in constantly shifting patterns and juxtapositions of colour. I spend hours recording these amazingly beautiful natural happenings with my camera. As I write this I have in front of me several photographs. One shows a fragment of down, afloat in liquid jade, sailing over a submerged leafy shape in soft, dark emerald. Another shows a red and purple fuchsia flower lying on a golden autumnal leaf. Around it are more leaves, half rotted, their skeletons revealed against a background that slides from viridian into turquoise and aquamarine. Translucent bubbles overlay some of the leaves as does the duckweed, its small oval shapes in the palest tea-green like the brush strokes of a pointillist painter. This humble pond is a gallery of ephemeral aquatic art and I could fill a gallery with photographs by way of praise and celebration.

Our rhubarb patch is another source of delight and wonder. Of all the plants in our garden it has the largest leaves – Leaves upon which rain can loudly drum or gently patter. People buy CDs of rain falling on leaves to help them relax and sleep. Just as calming is the way, in a wind, rhubarb sways and quietly creeks. I like to lie flat and peer between thick red, pink and purple columns; to look up and see the underside of the leaves backlit, their ribs and veins clearly defined. I am no rhubarbarian. I don't just eat it; I enjoy its superb architecture and structural engineering; and the way the sun shafts through holes in the canopy made by munching caterpillars, stippling stems and mottling moist shadows.

There is no wall where the end of the garden meets the shore. Instead there's a short stone-faced drop that forms a rampart. The height of it varies according to the extent to which storm winds and high seas have piled against it shoals of pebbles. At spring tide[2] high water the sea is no more than three or four feet away from the end of the garden, bringing with it a huge variety of rubbish, driftwood and dead seaweed. Plastics I remove and put in bin-bags. The rest is grist to the tumbling waves. Although my beachcombing is mostly confined to this strip of shore, the ocean's offerings are bountiful. Today I found two rings just big enough to fit on my little finger. One was a conical limpet shell, the top two thirds of which had been snapped off, leaving the frilly circular base with a hole in the middle. The other was the last quarter inch of the neck of a green beer bottle, its jagged edges long since smoothed away. I have become a seaglunter – a sea-glass hunter. Almost every week I add to my collection of curving, opalescent sea-gems in bottle greens and browns or almost clear, all slightly frosted and transformed. Once man-made objects, they have been claimed by nature. I include ceramics in my collection. The other day I found rounded pieces of blue-white willow pattern china lying among a heap of exactly matching empty mussel shells.

When the tide is far out at spring low tide a kelp jungle is exposed. This particular species of kelp is oarweed. Without the sea to support its weight, it lies in a tangled mass. When submerged, however, it becomes a swaying upright forest, designed to move with the waves as they crash onto the shore. Its flexibility allows it to survive in situations when more rigid plants would snap or be torn from the rock.[3] The Scottish Natural Heritage publication *Kelp Forests* says:

> The oarweed forest marks the junction between land and sea. It is probably one of the most natural environments that can be explored by a land dweller, in that, around most of Scotland, it is only rarely affected by human activity.

Early one morning, at low-tide and when the sun was newly risen and shining horizontally through this colony of kelp, I walked to the rocky outer margin of the inter-tidal zone. The kelp's thick wet gelatinous blades gleamed and glimmered in shades of brown ranging from amber to umber. On the underside of the blades, or among the stems, were sea slugs, squirts, sponges, small crabs, tiny five-armed starfish, sea anemones and a host of other miniature marine life that I could not name. Cautiously I manoeuvred across the slippery surface. Writhing shapes shone like luculent, pellucid gold – a magical kingdom existing for less than an hour before the sun rose higher and the turning tide hid it again.

Within a short walk from where I live many more adventures for the eye and mind await. There is always more to learn, more surprises, joy and wonder to encounter, fresh ways to grow. I have touched upon only a few. I have said nothing of the flowers, trees and bushes, the birds, bees and butterflies, the sunsets and cloudscapes; the sculpted driftwood, the seashells, the countless ways light falls upon, passes through or is reflected by an immense variety of surfaces. Step outside and almost immediately all five senses are fully engaged. Take any square meter of what lies immediately beyond my backdoor and a team of artists, botanists, biologists, micro-scientists and philosophers could write an entire volume on that alone. In experiencing the close and the small there is as much to be discovered as journeying to the far corners of the Earth. I do not need to travel great distances in order to reach new realms of the imagination, attain new heights of understanding and depths of feeling.

NOTES

1 From Helen Keller's poem 'The Song of the Stone Wall' (1910).

2 Spring tides occur twice a month just after a full moon or a new moon. At spring tides the tidal range is at its greatest, advancing up the beach to its highest point and receding down the beach to its lowest point. The name 'spring tide' comes from the notion of the tide 'springing forth', it has nothing to do with the season of the same name.

3 Seaweeds do not have roots (which draw nutrients from the soil). They have holdfasts, which act as anchors.

TWO SHETLAND POEMS

CLOUDBURST AT CULLIVOE

Kayaking to Cullivoe,
High-cliffed bay beckons, calls.
Sky splits, clouds burst. Heavy hail
Flattens a rude hooligan sea
To undulating prairie,
Completely pearl-encrusted
And sibilantly hissing.

Torrent-streaked cliff-face foams.
Grooves and gullies splash and gush.
Falls' fierce thunder fills the bay;
Edge-giddy drop, churning plunge.
Rainbow greets squall's sudden end.
Drainage roar of flooded land
Marks moon's passage through the night.

NAMELESS COVE

Small nameless cove unspoiled.
Stream, tidal pools, sea-caves,
In far corner of the world.
Grain-heavy grasses wave
Rippling in the wind.
Hear pebbled melody,
Where fat brown stippled trout find
Untroubled sanctuary.

Beneath orange moon I sleep,
Snug, safe from storm's sea fetch.

Precious memories I keep,
Otters playing on the beach;
Seals, unafraid, glide and turn,
Graceful in sea-green cove.
White shell sands stain pink at dawn,
Dear sweet nameless scene I love.

Ways to call cove get jotted down,
But I can't bear to see things tamed -
Things way beyond being owned.
Don't change! Please, please remain unnamed!
Praise be for unguided wander.
Ex marks the spot excites no pleasure.
Seek areas of the yonder
Where joyful wonder is the treasure.

THREE HAIBUN

I walk a narrow coastal track under miles of beech and oak. On my left, glimpsed through trees, a long sea loch stretches ahead. Sometimes it's way below; sometimes it's beside me, a companion, quietly lapping.

> beneath loch's surface
> palebarnacled skeleton
> wrecked hopes and dreams

Stands of gold and red flare like forest fires amongst the greens. Bark steams when touched by the long-fingered sun. But the sky is darkening.

> canyons, cliffs, mossed walls
> submerged in wooded gloom
> fathoms from the sky

As I follow a yellow-leaved path, my thoughts dwell on betrayals of long ago. In the last quarter of my life they still seethe in my blood.

> in the darkest part
> wild goats thrashes through thickets
> and disturbed birds squawk

My stride quickens as I fantasise revenge. Thunder, a growling tiger, roams the forest. The wind picks up.

> driven by the wind
> harried waves hurry to the land
> slap and smack the shore

Thunder recedes to a distant rumble. The wind abates as suddenly as it arose. Rain. Insistent rain which thwacks waxen leaves, splashes my skin and patters on my hood. Its steady drumming, its gentle passage through the branches sooths me, washing away my anger.

quietly dripping
renewing rain
seeps to waiting roots.

ACKNOWLEDGEMENTS

I am most grateful to the editors of all the publications wherein parts of this book, some in slightly different form, first appeared, and also to the authors and their publishers whom I have quoted, as acknowledged in the notes. Many of the scenes described took place in the company of friends. I would like to thank them for their part in these adventures, particularly my regular companion, Archie Sinclair. Huge thanks are due to my wife, Sallie, for proofreading and her support throughout the years in my writing endeavours; and finally, Jay Griffiths for her perceptive, sensitive and elegant foreword. Ian Spring designed the book and the cover which features an etching by Kirstie Behrens. Ian Spring and Calum Smith provided many of the illustrations. Many thanks to them.

'Beinn Ime by Moonlight' was first published in the *Scots Magazine* (March, 1979) and then in the anthology of mountain writing *The Winding Trail* edited by Roger Smith. 'Argonauts Of The Western Isles' won the Scottish Association of Writers' award for the best essay in 1979. 'River' was originally script for a 10-minute film/DVD I was commissioned to write in 2009 by the Dundee based artists Dalziel + Scullion. This was part of a longer film entitled *Speaking the Land*. The project was funded by Scottish Natural Heritage. The footage of the river in the film is of the River Minnoch in the Galloway Forest Park. The script was published in *EarthLines Magazine*, November 2012. 'My Golden Isle' was published in *Argonauts of the Western Isles*. Slightly different versions of the other poems have been read on Radio Clyde 1986/87. 'Wolf' was originally a script for a 22-minute film/DVD I was commissioned to write in 2011 by the Dundee based artists Dalziel + Scullion, who were making the film for Timespan Museum & Arts Centre, Helmsdale (part funded by Highlands & Islands Enterprise, and Creative Scotland). The script was published in *EarthLines* magazine in May 2013. 'Because It's Daft' was adapted from a chapter in my biography of W H Murray, *The Sunlit Summit* (Sandstone Press, 2013). This book won the Saltire Society's award for Research Book of the Year. 'Man is not Himself Only' was written for *EarthLines* magazine, 2014. 'A Kind of Homecoming' was written in 2014 for the Helensburgh Writers' Workshop publication *2014 a Year to Remember*, put together to celebrate the year designated as the Year of Homecoming. 'Three Haibun' was published on the website *Contemporary Haibun Online*, 2006. 'Two Shetland Poems was written in 2020 for my chapbook *ShoreLines*. 'Short Essays Close To Home', 'Near Is The New Far', 'The Kinetic Landscape' and 'In Praise of Rain' were all written for my blog *Autumn Voices* (www. autumnvoices.co.uk).